Somerset
CARNIVALS

Somerset CARNIVALS

A CELEBRATION OF FOUR HUNDRED YEARS

Roger Evans and Peter Nicholls

HALSGROVE

First published in Great Britain in 2005

**British Library Cataloguing-in-Publication Data.
A CIP record for this title is available from the British Library.**

ISBN 1 84114 483 5

HALSGROVE

Halsgrove House
Lower Moor Way
Tiverton, Devon EX16 6SS
Tel: 01884 243242
Fax: 01884 243325
E-mail: sales@halsgrove.com
Website: www.halsgrove.com

Printed and bound in Great Britain by CPI, Bath.

*Whilst every care has been taken to ensure the accuracy of the
information contained in this book, the publisher disclaims responsibility
for any mistakes which may have been inadvertently included.*

Contents

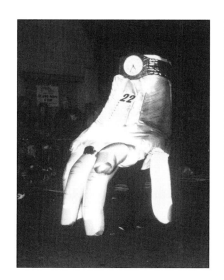 

From stone age to space age – Somerset celebrates with its winter carnivals.

Carnival – a Celebration of Four Hundred Years

Every 5 November, across the nation, something very strange occurs. Heads are craned skywards in search of exploding star bursts. Folks of all ages stare into the orange glow of huge bonfires, dentists schedule emergency appointments in their diaries for children who have chipped their teeth on hard-coated toffee apples. The sights and sounds of Bonfire Night are familiar to us all. But visit Somerset in November and you must be prepared to witness one of the world's best kept secrets. Somerset can boast the largest night time carnival processions anywhere in the world!

Mention carnival elsewhere and people think of the world famous Mardi Gras carnivals of Rio de Janeiro and New Orleans. Well, roll over Rio and kneel down New Orleans. Whilst these overseas events may internationally have a higher profile than our Somerset Carnivals, they are day time events. Our carnivals are by night, on a grander scale and spectacularly illuminated. Ours are beyond doubt the largest, most spectacular night time carnivals in the world.

So why are they not better known world wide, or even regionally. Well, the largest is Bridgwater Carnival. It is the first of the series of the 'Magnificent Seven', the Somerset Circuit. Under normal circumstances, the population of the town is around forty thousand. On carnival night it swells to a hundred and forty thousand. The town isn't capable of taking any more. There is no need for publicity on a global scale for such events, albeit they achieve global standards of entertainment. Across the county, approaching a million spectators already attend these giant parades. The towns can't take anymore.

There may be others more famous; there may be those where the price of entry suggests a major spectacle, but none compare with Somerset's Guy Fawkes Carnivals. The spectacular all-electric light-shows parade through the streets of the Somerset towns with lights glaring, music blaring and performers rhythmically swaying to the sounds of their chosen entries.

Eighty or so major floats, each with lighting

The Gunpowder Plot of 1605 is depicted on the leading float at Bridgwater Carnival. Nigel Holland, son of former carnival president Bill Holland, depicts Guy Fawkes.

SOMERSET CARNIVALS – A CELEBRATION OF FOUR HUNDRED YEARS

where the bulbs can be counted in the tens of thousands, form a procession which stretches out to a full two miles in length. Add to this the smaller entries and the walking entries. Nowhere in the world is there such a spectacle. But how did it all begin?

Remember, remember
The fifth of November
Gunpowder, treason and plot.
We see no reason
Why Gunpowder Treason
Should ever be forgot!

The answer lies in the words of the poem. It is to Guy Fawkes and the Gunpowder Plot of 1605 that

we must look for the origin of our famous winter carnivals.

It all began with the bonfires and burning effigies of Guy Fawkes and just grew from there. Today, Bridgwater and the other Somerset towns which form the Somerset Carnivals circuit, produce one of the largest spectacles in the world. For me, it has been a lifelong interest and involvement. For the carnival towns of Somerset it is a way of life, deeply rooted in their culture. It is in celebration of 400 years of the development of carnival that this publication has been produced. But first, let's look at the origins of the bonfires and the historic background to those events of four hundred years ago and then we'll look at the clubs of today.

Centurions Carnival Club's 1993 entry portrays the discovery and execution of Guy Fawkes.

PART 1

History and Background

A nation divided

Whilst the Somerset carnivals date back to the Gunpowder Plot and Guy Fawkes, the story begins well before 1605. In the sixteenth century, Henry VIII ruled supreme, this being the king famous for his six wives. He wanted a male heir to the throne and a succession of wives had failed to produce the required legitimate offspring. At the beginning of his reign, the nation was Roman Catholic. However, Henry VIII wanted to divorce his wife and re-marry. The Pope had denied Henry that right and so in 1534 Henry, infuriated by the decision from Rome, declared the Act of Supremacy. This made Henry independent of the Church of Rome and he declared himself to be the head of the Church of England. The nation was divided between those who felt their allegiance remained with Rome and those who believed their allegiance was to their King. It was a division which was to be at the root of religious and political unrest for centuries to come. There followed a period of persecution and strong anti-Catholic feeling, with many members of that faith being burnt at the stake.

Henry was succeeded by his son Edward Vl and his half sister Mary. She married King Philip ll of Spain, a staunch Roman Catholic. Persecution swung the other way and, until Mary's death in 1558, it was the Protestants who perished at the stake.

Elizabeth I followed and her reign lasted forty five years until 1603. She resurrected the Act of Supremacy and the Pope declared her a heretic. Under her rule, many priests and prominent Catholics were severely persecuted. The Catholic faith in England was tenaciously held together by French trained Jesuit priests. On the death of Elizabeth, the Catholics danced in the streets. They knew that James Vl of Scotland would soon become James I of England. He was the son of the Catholic Mary Queen of Scots and had promised a better life for the Catholics. In reality, his succession brought little benefit. He lacked the strength to influence Parliament. Penal laws outlawing the practice of Catholicism were increasing in severity and frequency.

Meanwhile, a group of English Catholics were fighting alongside the Spanish army. They had a dream, a vision of a Catholic England. If James I could be deposed, then they could help Spain to conquer England and ensure its Catholic future. They devised a plot and recruited Guy Fawkes to carry out the deed.

Guy Fawkes

His real name was Guido Fawkes, the son of Edward Fawkes, a notary or proctor of the ecclesiastical courts and advocate of the consistory court of the Archbishop of York. His mother was Edith Blake, the daughter of an eminent merchant and Aldermen of York. In 1568, his mother gave birth to a daughter, Anne, who survived just seven weeks. Two sisters followed Guy who both survived to marry in later life.

Guy was born in Stonegate, in the centre of York, on 13 April, 1570 and was baptised at St. Michael-le-Belfry, where his father was buried just eight years later in January 1578. It was St Peter's School in the Horse Fair which he attended in 1578 and there his early development may well have been formed by the Jesuit headmaster, John Pullen. The brothers John and Christopher Wright also attended the same school and were later to be involved in the yet-to-be-hatched Gunpowder Plot.

Guy's mother Edith, some nine years after the death of her husband, remarried into a Catholic family. Guy's stepfather, Dennis Bainbridge, almost certainly influenced his strong Catholic views and on reaching the age of twenty one, Guy Fawkes

Guy Fawkes.

converted what little was left of his inheritance into cash. Around 1593 he joined the Catholic forces fighting in Holland. There he served in the militia for twelve years under Archduke Albert of Austria, serving with the Spanish army. He was described as a tall and powerfully built man, sporting a bushy rufus beard, flowing moustache and a head of thick red-brown hair. His achievements in the field of battle had earned him a worthy reputation among his fellow soldiers. He was described as 'of excellent good natural parts, very resolute and universally learned… sought by all the most distinguished in the Archduke's camp for nobility and virtue… a man of great piety, of exemplary temperance, of mild and cheerful demeanour, an enemy of broils and disputes, a faithful friend, and remarkable for his punctual attendance upon religious observance.'

During that military spell, he became skilled in mining and the use of explosives, skills which he was to put to use later in the plot against James. Mining may seem an unconventional occupation for a military man to follow but it was a skill required when attacking fortress or similar strongholds.

Fawkes' tour of duty with the Duke came to an end on 16 February 1603. He was granted leave to go to Spain to enlighten King Philip II about the plight of the Catholic community in England. During this time he met up with his former school colleague, Christopher Wright, and between them they sought the Spanish king's support for an invasion of England upon the death of Queen Elizabeth. As a mission, it was a failure, but their cards were now face up on the table. That same year, Queen Elizabeth obliged and passed away. James VI of Scotland, as Elizabeth's closest relative, assumed the throne as James l of England.

On returning to Brussels, Guy Fawkes was informed that Thomas Wintour had been seeking him.

Plotting

It was 25 April the following year that Guy Fawkes arrived in England with Thomas Wintour. The following month, on 20 May, they were joined by Robert Catesby, Thomas Percy and John Wright, the other members of the Gunpowder Plot. They met at the Duck and Drake Inn in the Strand, London. Their mission was to blow up the House of Lords and, more importantly, King James I. The time chosen was that of the opening of Parliament when it was known the king would be in attendance. Guy Fawkes then went under cover and assumed an alias. He was now to be known as John Johnson, a servant to Thomas Percy.

In March 1605, the conspirators rented a cellar beneath the Parliamentary buildings and Guy Fawkes and his colleagues began to fill it with barrels of gunpowder. These were carefully concealed beneath iron bars and bundles of wood. On 18 October, he met with Catesby, Wintour and Francis Tresham. Tresham had been invited to join the group and he was to prove to be one recruit too many. The group discussed how Catholic members of the House of Lords could be persuaded not to attend on the day of the planned explosion. But this needed to be done without raising suspicions of a plot. One of the Lords was William Parker, Lord Monteagle. He was also Tresham's brother-in-law. Tresham sent Lord Monteagle an anonymous letter warning him not to be in Parliament on the day concerned.

The Conspirators *by Crispen van de Passe.*

Discovered

There were just ten days to go to the opening of Parliament when Monteagle, sitting down to dinner at the time, received the letter. It read:

My lord, out of the love I bear to some of your friends, I have a care for your preservation. Therefore I would advise you, as you tender your life, to devise some excuse to shift of your attendance of this Parliament, for God and man hath concurred to punish the wickedness of this time. And think not slightly of this advertisement but retire yourself into your country, where you may expect the event in safety, for though there be no appearance of any stir, yet I say they shall receive a terrible blow, the Parliament, and yet they shall not see who hurts them. This counsel is not to be condemned, because it may do you good and can do you no harm, for the danger is past as soon as you have burnt the latter: and I hope God will give you the grace to make good use of it, to whose holy protection I commend you.

Monteagle showed the letter to Robert Cecil, Lord Salisbury who then took steps which led to the discovery of the explosives and the trap was set to capture the conspirators.

As late as 30 October, Guy Fawkes, unaware of the leak, visited the cellars and ensured everything was in place. On 3 November, the gang met in London and were satisfied that it was safe to proceed. With the exception of Guy Fawkes, all the members of the plot had escape plans in place but it was Guy Fawkes who was to keep watch over the cellar and to light the fuse, drawing on his experience fighting on the continent. Once the mission was over, his next task was to return to the continent and spread the news.

On 4 November, members of the Lords were searching the cellars led by the Earl of Suffolk. A further search took place that evening led by Sir Thomas Knyvett. They spotted an exceptionally large pile beneath which were the hidden barrels. Guy Fawkes was there and when questioned, declared the "goods" to be the property of his master, Thomas Percy. Later that day, a little before midnight, they returned to the cellar, now convinced of the evil intent of Guy Fawkes. There they found and arrested him. On searching his person, they also found the materials to ignite the gunpowder and, beneath the bundles of wood and iron bars, they uncovered thirty six barrels of explosives. There was more than enough evidence of his treachery.

November 5th, 1605

In the early hours of the morning on 5 November, Guy Fawkes was taken to the king's bedchamber where the Privy Council had already gathered. Guy

Fawkes maintained his story that he was John Johnson, the servant of Thomas Percy. When questioned by the king as to his motive, he declared that 'dangerous diseases required dangerous remedies' and that his intentions had been to blow any Scots present (King James, for example) back over the border into Scotland.

On hearing of the capture of Guy Fawkes, Catesby and Thomas Wintour fled to the Midlands to meet the rest of their group in Warwickshire. For three days they moved from one safe house to another until, at Holbeche House in Staffordshire, Catesby, Percy and the Wright brothers were discovered and killed in the raid on the house. Thomas Wintour was taken to the Tower of London.

Meanwhile, Guy Fawkes was subjected to interrogation. On 6 November, the king wrote a letter declaring that 'The gentler tortures are to be used unto him, et sic per gradus ad mia tenditur [and thus by degrees increase to the worst], and so God speed your goode worke'. The laws of the country at that time stated that only the king or his Privy Council could sanction such torture.

Sir William Wade, Lieutenant of the Tower, set about his duties and the following day, under the stress of continuous violent interrogation, Guy Fawkes cracked, revealing his true identity and that five others were involved. A day later, he revealed the details of the plot but not the names of his fellow conspirators. After another day of extreme torture, on 9 November, he revealed names knowing that they had already been captured. His final confession bears witness to his poor state at the time of his signing, his signature being barely legible.

Execution

On 31 January 1606, Guy Fawkes was executed in the Old Palace Yard, Westminster. Percy and Catesby had already been shot as they tried to flee. Thomas Wintour, Ambrose Lockwood and Robert Keyes, all of whom had been found guilty of involvement in the conspiracy, were taken to the Old Palace Yard and hanged, drawn and quartered. Then came Guy Fawkes. Weakened from the days of torture, his suffering was soon to be over. So weak was he that the hangman had to assist him in ascending the ladder to the scaffold. When he dropped, his neck broke and he was spared the pain of live disembowelment. Next to the gallows the chopping block awaited the act of butchery as his body was quartered.

Whether his intentions were honourable or not, the name of Guy Fawkes lives on and it was Parliament itself which ensured its survival. In 1606 Parliament agreed that 5 November, from that day forth, should be a day of public thanksgiving for 'the the joyful day of deliverance'. The bonfire and firework tradition has survived ever since and the yeomen of the guard still carry out a ceremonial search of the Houses of Parliament an hour before any state opening.

Across London, bonfires were lit on which to burn effigies of the Pope. The practice of putting an effigy of Guy Fawkes on the top of the fire came later, as did the fireworks which we now associate with the occasion. Indeed at Lewes, on the Sussex coast, effigies of the Pope are still burned.

By 1607, the bonfire practice had spread across the nation and in parts of the country was to develop into the major events which we can witness today. The celebrations live on albeit perhaps the religious background and original cause for celebration are almost forgotten. Today there is a different cause. Those celebrations are now part of the very cultural life blood of many of the West Country communities. But more of that later.

Suffice it to say that Guy Fawkes today is cynically remembered as 'the only man ever to enter Parliament with honest intentions!' However, his attempt to reverse the persecution of Catholics backfired in the wake of the failed attempt to destroy the king and Parliament. The event had only further fanned the flames of anti-Catholic feeling and led to a significant increase in the harshness of anti-Catholic legislation.

Was there a local conspirator?

Robert Parsons was a Jesuit priest born in June 1546, the son of a Nether Stowey blacksmith, the middlemost of eleven children. He was raised as a Catholic and educated at Stogursey, Taunton and Balliol College, Oxford. In July 1575 he joined the Society of Jesuits and became a missionary four years later. He followed a life of mystery and intrigue, plotting and scheming against the Protestant authorities. In June 1579 he landed at Dover, disguised as a soldier, and thereafter followed an intense period of espionage. He was continually and unsuccessfully hunted by government agents who were unable to capture this elusive 'Pimpernel' character. As part of his cover, he used a number of aliases including that of Robert Cowbuck.

Much of his time was spent travelling around Europe, drumming up support and raising finances for the Spanish Armada. It is therefore quite possible, though with no proof of such, that he would have influenced the plans for the Gunpowder Plot. Parsons was never held to account for any of his espionage activities, albeit one of his closest friends was executed for his part in the plot, and Parsons certainly kept a low profile in the period following the capture of Guy Fawkes. It is alleged that he obtained the hangman's rope used for his friend's

execution and kept it until his death as a reminder, or perhaps as a penance. He was a close associate of Cardinal William Allen and together they plotted against the Protestant English monarchs, favouring an armed invasion by the continental Catholics. He died in April 1610 in Rome where he was serving the Pope as rector of the English Church. No one will ever know if he was involved in any way with the Gunpowder Plot but suffice it to say he was frequently in the right places at the right time.

Robert Parsons of Over Stowey.

An early tableau entry.
Courtesy Mrs Ena Hawkins

Bonfires and burning the Guy

Imagine centuries ago, the doom and gloom of those winter days when the nights were long and daylight hours correspondingly short. There were no street lights, no brightly lit shop windows. The dark of night was total darkness, a sensation we seldom experience today. The only heat was from open fires. The only light was from the fires or from torches made from animal fats. Imagine how depressing it could be during those dark evenings at the end of October knowing that the longest and coldest nights had yet to come. And then imagine the thrill and pleasure of a communal bonfire. Free light, free heat, food for all and a time for singing and dancing. Bonfires were a great way to put a bit of spirit back into a gloomy existence.

The tradition of bonfires goes back well before the 1605 Gunpowder Plot, but the Plot has certainly helped to keep the tradition alive. Even before the Romans came to Britain, the end of the year was celebrated with bonfires. In pagan times, 1 November, as we know it now, was New Year's Day. Bonfires were lit, torches carried in procession, sacrifices made and mistletoe, with its symbolism of fertility, played a useful role in livening up the celebrations.

The Celtic New Year was celebrated with the ancient festival of Samhain (pronounced sawm) with bonfires as the centrepieces. This tradition spread across the entire known world and formed an important part of those festivities. It was a time of year when decisions had to be made as to which animals to keep and feed through the winter, and which to slaughter. Hence it was a time of feasting and the bones left over would be put on a fire, hence bone fire became bonfire. When Christianity arrived in Britain, 1 November was named All Saints Day to validate its place in the Christian calendar. But what made those celebrations different in English communities was the addition of the burning of effigies of the Pope and then Guy Fawkes from 1606 onwards.

Today the tradition of Guys survives especially within the junior community. Youngsters create Guys from old clothing, stuffed with rags or paper, and then beg 'A penny for the Guy', the proceeds normally going to the purchase of fireworks. But across the nation, the importance of the Guys was in throwing them onto the 5 November bonfire and thus celebrating annually the failure of Guy Fawkes to blow up Parliament. It may seem a tasteless comparison but I well remember the news broadcasts in the wake of the 11 September attack on the Twin Towers in New York. Television took us into the towns and villages of Afghanistan and Pakistan where extremists were celebrating America's disaster by burning the Stars and Stripes in the street. Likewise effigies of George W. Bush were put to the torch by excited, exuberant crowds of fanatics. These were the religious extremists, perhaps unrepresentative of the population as a whole. Nonetheless, those events, broadcast worldwide, provided an insight into how major events with religious undertones can be celebrated with such fervour. In their own way, they reflected those seventeenth-century celebrations much closer to home when the nation was divided on religious grounds and the failure of the Gunpowder Plot was celebrated with bonfires and the burning of effigies.

As late as the early 1800s, Guy Fawkes Night was still called Pope's Day but the focus was well and truly on the Guy. The traditional way to build the Guy was to take old clothing and stuff it with straw. To complete the image, a mock up lantern was placed in one hand and a bunch of matches in the other. The Guy would then be carried through the town, seated on a kitchen chair, until its time came to go on the bonfire.

The Living Guy

There is an amazing account from around two hundred years ago of a living Guy. William Hone's The Everyday Book of 1827 tells the story.

On the fifth of November, a year or two ago, an outrageous sparkle of humour broke forth. A poor hard-working man, while at breakfast in his garret, was enticed from it by a message that some one who knew him wished to speak to him at the street door.

'Spare a copper for the Guy, sir.' The Fifth of November by L. A. G. Strong (1937).

When he got there he was shaken hands with, and invited to a chair. He had scarcely said "nay" before "the ayes had him," and clapping him in the vacant seat, tied him there. They then painted his face to their liking, put a wig and paper cap on his head, fastened a dark lantern, in one of his hands, and a bundle of matches in the other, and carried him about all day, with shouts of laughter and huzzas, begging for their "Guy". When he was released at night he went home, and having slept upon his wrongs, he carried them the next morning to a police office, whither his offenders were presently brought by warrant, before the magistrates, who ordered them to find bail or stand committed. It is illegal to smug a man for 'a Guy'.

A Cruickshank sketch from William Hone's 1827 The Every-Day Book.

Scary days! Another reference from the same publication refers to the year 1433.

At the same period, the butchers in Clare-market had a bonfire in the open space of the market, next to Bear-yard, and they thrashed each other 'round about by the woodfire, with the strongest sinews of slaughtered bulls. Large parties of butchers from all the markets paraded the streets, ringing peals from marrow-bones and cleavers, so loud as to overpower the storms of sound that came from the rocking belfries of the churches…'

And therein lies a reference to the practice of ringing the church bells as part of the celebrations.

Variations on the bonfire

Accounts from all around Britain reflect a similar pattern of celebration. In London, Guys were paraded through the streets in the 1850s, some as small as a doll, others 15 feet high. In Exeter in the 1820s,

hundreds of youngsters used to assemble, letting off squibs and crackers. At about 4 a.m. on the 5th, the inhabitants were reminded of the evening's amusements by the firing of cannons from various parts of the city. After breakfast, guys of various kinds, large and small, were carried about in order to obtain money. Youngsters had small guys, about the size of dolls; the large guys sometimes had a lantern suspended from one arm and a bundle of brimstone matches from the other arm…

Across the nation, communities celebrate 5 November in many different ways. In Ottery St Mary, each of Ottery's public houses sponsors a tar barrel. These barrels, in the weeks leading to the big event, are soaked in tar. On the night, each barrel is lit in turn outside of its pub. Once the flames have taken a good hold, they are hoisted onto the backs of locals who support them on their shoulders. A number of barrels are lit over the course of the evening, gradually increasing in size. This same sight could once have been witnessed in our Somerset towns and such events are well documented particularly for Glastonbury, where lighted barrels were rolled down the High Street to the bonfire at the market cross, and Bridgwater, where they were either rolled from the premises from which they emerged or carried head high to the Cornhill bonfire.

We must now be careful not to read any religious or even historic significance into our modern day carnivals. The Bridgwater procession is always led off by a float depicting the Gunpowder Plot with Guy Fawkes and his conspirators. But for the public who view the procession, there is nothing else to remind them of any religious significance. Having said that, in Bridgwater, as late as 1850, a giant effigy of the Pope was paraded through the streets and ceremoniously thrown on the bonfire. Certainly there are communities in the British Isles that still burn effigies of the Pope on Bonfire night. In the Sussex town of Lewes, there is great rivalry between the five bonfires societies to produce the best Bonfire Night celebrations. A number of Guys are produced by the various competitors, some of which are enormous. These effigies frequently portray the Pope or currently unpopular political figures, Prime Ministers or Presidents, according to the flavour of the month. In recent years, Margaret Thatcher, Bill Clinton, Osama Bin Laden, George W Bush and even Winnie the Pooh have been depicted, the latter as a

Cornhill Bonfire circa 1900.

protest against the pursuance by the Disney corporation for the full character rights of A. A. Milne.

The origin of the Lewes celebration dates back to the years before the Gunpowder Plot when, in the 1550's Queen Mary launched a campaign against the Protestant Church. Two hundred and twenty eight protestants were burnt at the stake. Seventeen of these executions were in Lewes and therein lies the fervour and the passion behind the Lewes bonfires. Most of those executed were punished after they were discovered saying prayers in English rather than Latin. Later came the Gunpowder Plot and since then the Pope most frequently depicted at the Lewes bonfires is Pope Paul V, the incumbent Pope in 1605. By 1679, the celebrations had developed into an elaborate procession with people dressed in military and clerical costumes.

By around 1800, the Lewes Bonfire Boys had developed the celebrations into a fairly riotous affair. Blazing tar barrels were dragged through the streets and a local firework, the Rouser was hurled into the crowds. Arrests for riotous and dangerous behaviour were frequent with the offenders often finishing up in prison. On one occasion, one hundred London policemen were drafted in and the Riot Act was read to the crowd. In 1853 the Cliffe and Lewes Borough Bonfire Societies were

formed and thereafter the occasion became more organised. In many ways, Bridgwater's development has paralleled that of the history of the Lewes celebration, each with their own unique character developing.

Fireworks

It was the Chinese who were the first to develop fireworks as far back as two thousand years ago. They still form a significant part of celebrations in that country. On a recent trip there I was surprised by the frequency at which we would hear fireworks especially in the rural areas. I now realise that their use is standard practice for weddings, birthdays and other celebrations.

But when did fireworks arrive in Britain? It was a Somerset man who provides the earliest record of the use of gunpowder. Roger Bacon, born in Ilminster in 1214, became a Franciscan monk, linguist, alchemist and mathematician. He carried out chemical experiments in which he combined charcoal, sulphur and saltpetre. In 1242 he recorded that, if you know how to do it, you can light it and produce 'thunder and lightening'. It was probably the fourteenth-century crusaders, a hundred years later, who brought back fireworks as we would recognise them today. By 1486 they were being used for state occasions such as the wedding of Henry VII. Queen Elizabeth appointed a 'Fire master of England' and James II knighted his fire-master, so pleased was he with the display at his coro-nation. Thus fireworks had arrived and became an integral part of the 5 November celebrations.

As early as the first decades of the nineteenth century, young lads would use their Guys to beg for money with which to buy fireworks. Crackers and bangers were always popular with the youngster. In my own early days, it was the bangers which we purchased rather than rockets or sparklers. The bangers would be lit and then thrown as grenades. Those on the receiving end would rush forward to place a well aimed boot on the firework before it exploded. The whole exercise was full of bravado and we came to little harm – at least until we were introduced to rook scarers. These were brought into the town by the young lads of the farming communities. Rook scarers were used in the fields to protect the crops. A long slow burning fuse connects a series of these larger than average fire-works together such that they would ignite at regular intervals during the day, sounding just like a twelve bore shot gun.

My introduction to these devices came when it was my turn to rush forward and step on a 'banger' hurled our way. I arrived just in time – and then it exploded beneath my foot and I was deaf for the next three days! It wasn't a banger but a Rook Scarer. My mother met with a similar disaster whilst watching the Bridgwater Carnival procession. As late as the 1950s, it was still common practice to throw fireworks into the crowd. Hence all those who attended, wore their oldest clothing on the assumption that a firework would burn a hole in whatever they wore before the night was out. In my mother's case, the firework thrown into our part of the crowd flew straight into her Wellington boot and therein it exploded. Treatment at the hospital was called for and her leg was black and blue for weeks after. In the years that followed, the practice of throwing fireworks was made an offence and the carnival became a much safer event. The hospital treated 65 people for burns that evening.

The Cornhill Bonfire of 1904.

PART 2

Introducing Bridgwater

Whilst the Guy Fawkes celebrations were common across the country, in Bridgwater they evolved in a special way. Seventeenth-century Somerset was mainly Protestant and perhaps for that reason the Guy Fawkes celebrations were at least as enthusiastic as elsewhere. But in addition, Bridgwater was a trade centre, a working town and sea port, the kind where bonfire celebrations were particularly well received. As the centuries progressed, the carnival revelries took on a shape and culture of their own and the religious undertones were forgotten.

Cornhill Bonfire

For Bridgwater, it all began with a huge bonfire at the Cornhill in the town centre. The bonfire was larger here than anywhere else in the town. It was huge, at least twenty four feet across the base. Along the quaysides, the sea-going ships would moor up on the seaward side of the town bridge, with river barges mooring on the other. All kinds of small craft were used and these small boats were pitched in tar to keep them watertight. As they reached retirement, so one or more would form part of the foundation of the November bonfire. To that would be added as many as a hundred old tar barrels. So strong was the tradition of using old boats for the foundation of the fire, that as the river trade diminished and old boats became scarer, it was not unusual for perfectly serviceable boats to be 'acquired' without the owners' permission. The theft of small boats became a seasonal problem, only occurring around the early days of November. And so it became necessary to mount a guard around the dock at that time of year. Other unusual items often found their way to the bonfire and one year included a piano. One imagines that with such a foundation, any bonfire is going to burn bright and long. In the latter years of the bonfire, it may be safe to assume that it was much better organised since we know that the lighting of it was arranged by the vicar of St Mary's.

In 1847 Richard Chedzoy and James Duckham foolishly threw tar barrels, which were not empty onto the bonfire. As the burning pitch melted, like molten lava, it poured from the barrels and flowed towards shop premises in the town centre. The two men were arrested and tried. Found guilty and unable to pay their 50 shilling fines, they spent the next six weeks in gaol at Wilton, being released just in time for the Christmas Festivities.

Opinions differ on when the bonfire was lit.

Some reports refer to the fire being lit at 7.00 p.m. whilst others declare it was never lit until the procession had passed. Whatever time it started, the revelries went on well past midnight. To get the fire started, something like fifteen gallons of paraffin were thrown onto the bonfire and a group of young lads with tapers alight would approach and ignite the fire. This was not a particularly safe practice since the initial burst of flames would shoot some two hundred feet into the air and could allegedly be seen from South Wales. The heat was so intense that the nearby shops would board up their windows and hang wet tarpaulins over them to prevent damage.

The Cornhill bonfire was not the only one in the town, but it was the one around which the procession centred, and as will be described later, was the one which triggered the procession in the very early years of the celebration.

On occasions the bonfire was used as a way for groups to publicly express their anger with individuals who it was felt had let down the community. In 1860 an effigy was produced of a worker from the carriage works. It appears this fellow had brought about the dismissal of a number of his colleagues, who took their revenge by parading his effigy, labelled 'A traitor to his shop mates', through the streets before committing him to the flames of the Cornhill bonfire. In 1867, in similar fashion, a farmer titled 'The King of Dunwear' was given the same treatment in this nineteenth-century equivalent of 'Naming and Shaming'.

In 1872, the Cornhill bonfire was host to the effigy of someone called the Yard Spy, presumably a reference to a tell-tale brickyard worker; the Salmon Parade bonfire was host to Brother B and Sister S, a widower and seaman's wife accused of an extra marital relationships and the Barclay Street and Albert Street fires each consumed an effigy of alcoholic and unfaithful wives, one with a gin bottle suspended around its neck declaring its part in the unseemly behaviour of the miscreant. This list only provides part of the roll call of bonfires held around the town, there being at least as many again not mentioned here. Even as late as 1906, an effigy of the minister of the Baptist Church was committed to the flames. He had unsuccessfully attempted to stop the pubs opening late on carnival night! What a contrast to the 1946 vicar of St Mary's Church who referring to the carnival procession in his Sunday morning service told the congregation how he was so impressed, he went home and went down on his knees to thank God that he lived in such an age as this.

The final bonfire

Alas the bonfire, which for so long was the focal point for the carnival celebrations in Bridgwater, is no longer with us. The last bonfire took place on 6 November, 1924. In charge of proceedings was Edwin Scribbens who had been a 'bonfire boy' for sixty one years. Harry Burge led a procession of bonfire boys around the stack of material, each holding a lighted taper. And then at the appointed hour, the tapers were applied and, with a huge whoosh and a rocketing flame, the last Cornhill bonfire had been lit. It was a year when the Eastenders Carnival Club took first place with their tableau Rupert Emperor of Estoria and Imperial Court. With that success, they were presented with the Kerr Cup, a new trophy introduced that year and still the one that Bridgwater clubs strive to win today.

The following year Trinidadian Asphalt was laid on the roads around the town centre. Whilst this made travel much easier, it was unfortunately a material which would burn quite well especially beneath bonfires! On 28 August, 1925, the carnival committee met at the Golden Ball in the High Street to discuss what to do. The total impracticality of a huge bonfire on the asphalt surface was recognised. Attempts were made to move the bonfire elsewhere, away from the town centre, in order to maintain the tradition. But the new site lacked the atmosphere and consequently the support of the people. By now, however, the carnival procession was sufficiently well established that it had become the centre of focus and survived to go from strength to strength. Indeed, the removal of the bonfire from the celebrations perhaps helped to push the carnivalites on to bigger and better things now that their energies were more directed towards their procession entries rather than the fire itself.

Whilst the bonfire lasted until 1924, there were attempts to kill it off much earlier. During the 1870s the number of visitors to Bridgwater had swelled considerably, the railway network allowing spectators to arrive from Weston, Bristol, Taunton and Glastonbury. In 1880, by which time the crowds were now quite considerable, there was an incident when the bonfire was still blazing an hour after midnight and a large supply of burning material still lay behind the railings of the Cornhill dome waiting to be added to the fire. Several hundred revellers were still enjoying the evening when the newly formed fire brigade were called in to extinguish the fire.

This was not well received. Fighting broke out. An axe was taken from the back of one of the fire-pumps and used to chop one of the two hoses. We know that the other hose survived the ordeal since it is recorded that the carnivalites then turned that hose onto the firemen themselves. Captain George Ricks, who was in charge of the fire crew, was at the scene with the town crier, Jack Fackrell. The presence of the town crier indicates the serious nature of the occasion since it was the town crier's responsibility to read the Riot Act should matters get out of hand. Meanwhile, Captain Ricks saw how one of his firemen, James Ware, had been physically attacked by the angry crowd. Ware managed to escape and hid in the town crier's house in Clare Street. There the crowd threw various missiles at the windows and tried to break down the door despite the police guard. Ware managed to escape again and this time was chased, by a crowd of some two hundred and fifty people, to his house in Dampiet Street where the missile throwing was repeated and his windows broken. Totally outnumbered, the police had been powerless to intervene. By 3.00 a.m. life had returned to normal.

The incident had highlighted the passion around the local custom of carnival and demonstrated how difficult it would be to impose any sort of change. Part of the problem for the authorities was that the event was a spontaneous affair lacking in formal organisation. There was no one to whom the authorities could go to discuss better arrangements. The following year, the first carnival committee was formed and through the 1880s a banner was carried aloft at the head of the procession declaring 'Loyalty, Fraternity, Jollity.' That original committee was formed under the leadership of Captain W. J. Ford, JP, a former army officer and the manager of the local bank, described as a fine specimen of the old English gentleman with a long beard and black velvet jacket. The result was the first organised procession. All the participants had been notified in advance to gather at the railway station. There Captain Ford and his band organised the procession which paraded through the town to the Cornhill, Penel Orlieu, St Mary Street, George Street and back to the Cornhill and the site of the bonfire. The spectators loved it. The performers dispersed, returned to their headquarters in the various pubs, only to return later with their squibs and coshes to continue the spectacle. The night had been an outstanding success and its importance in the history of Somerset carnivals cannot be exaggerated.

From that time on, the carnival has been officially and competently organised. Amongst the many who have been honoured with the presidency of the organisation was Sammy Woods from 1902 to 1905. Sammy had been born in Australia but emigrated to England partly for a university education. Somehow he ended up in Bridgwater learning the brewing trade. He was a tremendous all-round sportsman with an incredible list of international honours. He was a Cambridge Blue at cricket and rugby. In 1886 he played cricket for Australia and two years later was playing for England. He also represented England at rugby.

Squibbing in Bridgwater's High Street.

I mentioned earlier John Fackrell, the Town Crier. There was another occasion when his services were called upon. It was a year when the rain on the day of the procession came as a deluge and lasted for hours. Fackrell was instructed to do the rounds of the town announcing a twenty-four-hour postponement of the celebrations. Before he had completed the circuit, the skies cleared. Fackrell then went back around his route declaring that the carnival was now back on and the procession went ahead as originally planned.

Squibbing

One traditional activity which sets Bridgwater Carnival apart from the rest is the tradition of squibbing. The squibs are giant fireworks which are attached to coshes. Coshes are something like a large sweeping brush with no bristles. Where the bristles would otherwise be, a large cylindrical firework, the squib, is lashed into place. Once lit, the cosh is held in both hands by the squibber, like a weightlifter's bar, and kept aloft above head height, with the squib pointing skywards, until it finally expires with a loud retort.

In truth, for health and safety reasons, the squibs these days are much smaller than their latter-year counterparts. Nonetheless the squibbing event is an outstanding spectacle as over one hundred carnivalites form two lines the length of Bridgwater's High Street and simultaneously ignite their Bridgwater Squibs. It is an amazing sight as the sparks shoot forth from a hundred or more fireworks reaching to well above rooftop height. The spectacle culminates in a hundred explosive reports as the squibs one by one expire, with the crowd always giving an enormous cheer to the one which survives the longest.

Once the squibbing is over, all there is left to do is for the crowd to stand outside of the Town Hall awaiting the all-important results to be announced declaring the winners of the procession which took place earlier in the evening, results which then set the pace for the rest of the big series of seven major Somerset carnivals.

Early disasters

The squibbing tradition possibly goes back to the early 1600's but at least to 1716 and an incident with John Taylor. He was a local manufacturer of the squibs but the event is recorded only because of the tragic circumstances surrounding his name. It appears that Taylor failed to take the necessary precautions in handling the explosives and managed to blow up himself and two of his children.

The practice of making fireworks was carried out in many homes and gave the local authority great cause for concern. A similar but less tragic incident occurred in Mr Stacey's shop in 1865.

Three young lads were grinding powder to make squibs. A quantity of powder was spilt and fell over the mill. Unwisely one of the boys took a lighted taper to see how much had been spilt and where. The question became academic as the powder ignited. Three young lads, with minor injuries and smoke burns, walked out through the front of the shop – which no longer existed!

The traditional squibs were very simple affairs. They varied in size, up to two inches in diameter and twenty two inches long. The case, made of rolled up paper, was drawn in one inch from the top to form a choke of half an inch diameter. As the squib burned, this choke widened increasing the size of the illuminated area as it went. Various forms of metal and glass filings were mixed with gunpowder in varying proportions but typically totalling three pounds in weight. The bottom end of the squib was then packed with two ounces of rock powder to give the final loud report.

In 1892 a Chief Inspector from the Home Office visited the town and declared that the practice of making home-made squibs was illegal. He threatened the carnival committee that he would fine them £100 per day for each day that illegal fireworks continued to be manufactured in the town. The committee's response was to declare the end of the carnival. The carnival community had a different attitude. They distributed posters advertising the forthcoming event and declaring that only Bavarian squibs would be used and not locally made ones. Everyone knew what was meant by 'Bavarian'. The carnival continued and a minor revolution took place within the committee.

Prior to 1881, squibs were let off spontaneously throughout the day as and when the owners felt the urge. Smaller fireworks were often hurled indiscriminately into the crowd. The formation of an official committee helped to control and organise this element of the festivities into a popular public spectacle. The committee squibs were purchased from reputable suppliers and brought with them a higher cost than the home made ones. Since the clubs at the time squibbed in competition with each other, they preferred to make their own squibs to ensure that theirs were the biggest and the best. Consequently it was some while before proper control over the manufacture of squibs became common practice. Competition squibbing, where each club provided a team of squibbers who provided 'synchronised' squibbing, lasted until 1972 when Ramblers became the last club to win the Winslade Cup for the squibbing competition. Indeed I took part in one myself before the competition aspect was dropped in favour of being able to complete the evening's revels an hour or so earlier. If the procession suffered from hold ups and the squibbing took longer than expected, the last club to compete would at times be squibbing after one o'clock at night.

Squibbers of old performed in their costumes.

But back to the 1900s when the illegal, but bigger and better squibs were still home made. Fearing a repetition of the John Taylor disaster, in 1909 a raid took place on the home of Mr W. H. Kitch in Angel Crescent. There the Inspector of Explosives, assisted by the Borough Police Force and a search warrant, found 164 squibs weighing over a third of a ton. Each squib was 2 feet in length and weighed 7 pounds. Other paraphernalia was found; 39 pounds of gunpowder and a coffee mill to grind it; iron fillings; a ram rod; the roller and paper to make the squib cases. The evidence presented by the Town Clerk for the prosecution on the following Monday was overwhelming and appeals to release the materials went unheeded. The court heard how, if an explosion had taken place, not only would the garden shed in which they found the material have been destroyed, but the whole of Angel Crescent including its residents.

This particular haul had belonged to just one gang and included all the equipment needed to produce these enormous squibs. The guilty householder was fined £10 with £3 1s 6d costs and told how irresponsible he had been in putting the lives of so many people at risk. In the true spirit of carnival, a collection was taken to pay his fine and totalled £18 1s 6d. The £5 surplus was donated to the Soup Kitchen. The police agreed to release the confiscated squibs on the understanding that they were used for a public display to raise funds for the hospital. Unfortunately the squibs had been stored in a damp area with the result that the spectators were nearly suffocated with smoke.

Last minute problems

The committee squibs of today are much safer as a result of stringent changes in relation to the use of explosives. The committee however leave nothing to chance and each year a sample of the squibs to be used are tested to ensure they perform to a safe standard. This practice dates back to 1987 when a serious problem occurred with that year's supply.

The manufacturers had delivered the specifically manufactured squibs on time and they were secured in a safe place. A limited number were released to local PTAs for use at the school bonfires with carnivalites present to ensure their safe firing. Reports came back, however, detailing how four out of the five had exploded abnormally blowing the heads off the wooden coshes.

I was chairman of the carnival committee at the time and working in Canada. I flew back to help resolve the problem. Samples were taken from the main batch and fired. Sure enough, some of those exploded almost as soon as they were lit. They had proven to be unsafe for use in a public place or anywhere else.

I contacted the manufacturer and described the symptoms. The following day the unsafe squibs were taken away and replaced with ones which were guaranteed safe. The owners of the firework company, a father and son partnership, had worked through the night to ensure the show went on. Naturally we tested a sample from the delivery, a practice which has been continued ever since.

There is unfortunately a sad ending to this tale. That same year, whilst working on another customer's fireworks, something must have caused a spark in the building where the son of the same business was working. The whole building went up in a ball of flame as the explosive materials ignited. Unbeknown to me, the son had lost his life and my enquiry to the company the following year was answered simply by a photocopy of the local newspaper report describing the disaster. History was repeating itself some two hundred and seventy years after the John Taylor incident.

Unbroken tradition

Whilst we may boast that our carnivals have a continuous tradition dating all the way back to 1605, sceptics may claim this is not so. Indeed through the war years, there were no bonfire celebrations, so perhaps the claim of celebrating continuously for four hundred years lacks validity. But no, a hero comes to the rescue. During those dark years of the Second World War, a Bridgwater carnival character nicknamed 'Nosey' Lockyer walked the route each 'should have been' carnival night, bearing a torch in order to maintain the unbroken period of celebration. And his son Ted also inherited the carnival tradition for he became a founder member of the Gremlins Carnival Club; and his grandson Bev Lockyer is currently a members of Wills Carnival Club, as is his great granddaughter Fiona Lockyer, giving us another example of continuing traditions, that of the inheritance of carnival through the family generations.

Although carnival clubs may come and go, the overwhelming majority of clubs are at least thirty years old, albeit most of those surviving are post war clubs. But what happened during those war years? When the 'boys came home' from the last war, the carnival carried on where it had left off. The partly made costumes were brought out and finished. Many had to be altered, the owners having put on a few inches over the period of the six years during which the nation was at war. Others, owned by those who never returned, were passed on to new members.

The first carnival after the war was celebrated with greater delight than many before. The crowds turned out in record numbers. There was a bus shelter on the Cornhill popularly known as the 'cowshed'. It was used by scores of youngsters as a grandstand to afford a better view of the proceedings. Unfortunately, and unexpectedly, it collapsed under the pressure causing those on top to descend more rapidly than expected onto those watching below. The ambulance service treated over one hundred casualties that night, many of them from burns since the practice of throwing fireworks indiscriminately into the crowd was still rife.

It was a difficult period for clubs. The years of conscription had taken the young men of the town away from their cultural roots and into National Service, just at the time when they were most likely to become involved in the carnival tradition. The 1960s saw the end of conscription and with it the resurgence of the enthusiasm for carnival. The tradition grew from strength to strength, to its strong

Mike Crocker of Bridgwater safety checking a sample from a new batch of Bridgwater squibs.

present day position and giving us the world's most spectacular night time carnival.

Whilst the competition is fierce between the clubs, the camaraderie is equally strong. In times of trouble, they will always help each other out. The show comes first, the individual clubs second. One glowing example of this was when the Renegades Carnival Club, of which I am a founder and life member, had their float destroyed in an arson attack just a few nights before the grand procession. The fire had left little more than the chassis and wheels. Every single club in the town, and many from outside, rallied to the cause. Money was donated, electrical items handed over, materials arrived from around the county and a multitude of members and helpers from other clubs pitched in with just three nights to go. When the show went on the road, the entry was not far short of the original expectations and the response from the public was overwhelming.

Changing traditions

Over the years, the date on which the carnivals have been held have varied. For most of the county carnivals, the dates have revolved around the dates set by Bridgwater. Originally, the Bridgwater carnival was always on 5 November unless that was a Saturday or Sunday. However, as the procession became larger and the crowds swelled correspondingly, there was a need for traders to board up their shop windows to prevent crowd pressure from pushing them in. In 1909, the traders persuaded the committee that the carnival should be held on the Thursday nearest 5 November, Thursday being early closing day. That gave them Thursday afternoon to board up their shop windows. That situation continued for several decades, but it was not the long standing tradition that many people believed it to be.

A few years ago, the Bridgwater committee took the decision to move the event to the Friday nearest 6 November. This was in part to allow more families to attend, there being no school the following morning. Ideally they would have preferred to go for the Saturday but there was a huge public backlash to any proposed change. Another reason for change, and equally an argument against change, was that the day after Bridgwater Carnival had become an event in its own right, popularly known as Black Friday. Historically it was the day when the carnivalites let their hair down and celebrated with the winning club. It was a day of serious drinking after months of hard work. But it was well managed and controlled, and it was behind locked doors. The police turned a blind eye knowing how hard the members of the carnival community had worked and knowing the celebrations would be well contained. Unfortunately, with the relaxation of licensing hours, the event became an all day binge involving a far wider community than that of the carnivalites. The town was developing a bad name. Indeed, older members of the community would avoid going into the town on Black Friday.

And so, the carnival was controversially moved to the Friday which deprived the clubs of their opportunity to celebrate the following day because that is the day of North Petherton Carnival. Now the celebration takes place on the Sunday nearest 8 November and is known variously as 'the Black Sabbath' or 'Sad Sunday'.

Far less controversial have been the occasional changes to the route. In my early days, the procession lined up in the vicinity of the railway station, using St John Street and Wellington Road. These days it is difficult to get a car down Wellington Road let alone a carnival float. And so in 1975, the line up area was moved to Parkway, a length of dual carriageway almost a mile long and giving ample space in which to collect the floats into their numbered positions. The contrast between the old and new areas for lining up could not be greater and reflects the massive increase in both the size and number of floats over the last forty years.

At the other end of the town, the procession at one time went through North Street turning left into Northfields, a difficult corner at the best of times and one which frequently required the tractors and trailers to uncouple in order to complete the turn. Once the dual carriageway of Broadway opened, it provided an obvious safer alternative. Some years ago there was a controversial proposal, coming from the local constabulary, to change the procession route such that the floats would form up on the Bristol Road, travel through the Wylds Road Industrial Estate, over the Black Bridge, past the police station, into Penel Orlieu and then disperse along the Broadway. This would have been disastrous in terms of loss of atmosphere and the backlash to the proposal was enormous. Common sense was fortunately allowed to prevail.

There was an occasion when the traditional route was not adhered to, but just for the one year. Robert Washer, twice mayor of Bridgwater, had been a life-long supporter of carnival. One particular year, he was too ill to attend, indeed he was laid up in hospital, and so the committee arranged that the procession should take a detour in order to go past the hospital and let Bob see his carnival after all.

Another change of tradition has been the gradual introduction of grandstand seating. This provides a useful source of revenue for the organising committee and a safe and cosy way for spectators to watch the procession in some comfort. Over the years the benefits of this comfortable seating have been recognised by an increasing number of the public and additional stands are added each year to keep pace with the demand.

PART 3
Evolution of Carnival

Thus far, I have mentioned little of the carnival processions but it is important to realise first of all how the bonfires and the use of effigies of Guy Fawkes, the Guys, contributed to the development of the spectacle we witness today. It was the practice across the country to put the effigies of Guy Fawkes on the bonfire. In Bridgwater's town centre however, perhaps as a result of the high concentration of drinking houses, it became more competitive. Most of the local pubs had a 'gang' which would produce a Guy. On the evening of 5 November, these would be brought out into the street and carried aloft to the applause of the spectators. The one receiving the best response was adjudged by popular opinion to be the best for that year. In time, the number of Guys increased and it became necessary to mount them on horse drawn carts. Once again popular reaction was used to determine the winner.

In order to be more competitive, some of the gangs produced Guys which no longer resembled Guy Fawkes but instead wore the costume of a king or perhaps the national dress of some foreign land. These were clearly more popular with the public and in time the Guys disappeared to be replaced by wooden cut out models. The members of the gangs took to dressing themselves up in costumes and would masquerade around their entry adding colour, life and vitality. The presence of these masqueraders was essential since they carried the paraffin or powder torches which were used to illuminate the mounted entries.

Paraffin torches

The paraffin torches were constructed using a tin can which was fixed at the bottom end to a poll and with a slot at the other end through which poked out a wick. The inside was packed with wadding to hold the paraffin. Once lit, they were large enough to burn for several hours. For decades during the 1900s, the fee for carrying such a torch was 6d. Larger, double headed torches justified 9d for the bearer. It was quite tiring work bearing these torches for hours at a time and the bigger and older lads, greedy for the 9d, often took unfair advantage of those less experienced. The young inexperienced lads would offer to carry the large double torches. As they got closer to the end of the procession, so their arms would get tired and it was here the 'kind-hearted' experienced lads stepped in. They would wait near the finishing line and offer their help to the youngsters and then carry the torch for what remained of the route. Of course, the torch bearers were paid when they crossed the finishing line. It only took the inexperienced one year to learn the pattern of behaviour.

From those early days, the gangs and features as we see them today have evolved, the gangs displaying their unmoving tableaux and the features bringing song and movement to the spectacle. Understanding this background explains also why the floats are locally referred to as carts and the light bulbs are still referred to as lamps, maintaining those cultural linguistic links with the past.

An early walking entry at Bridgwater Carnival – Rickshaw and Passenger.

So we have the beginnings of the evolution of the procession. It all began with the bonfire, with effigies of Guy Fawkes being thrown into the flames. Then the production of the Guys became competitive. They were bedecked in costumes and paraded on carts. In the early days, they were still thrown on the bonfire. Then masqueraders joined the scene, resplendent in their costumes. And so the procession became part of Bridgwater culture.

It is impossible to tell just when the procession became a 'serious' affair rather than a spontaneous and disorganised display. Journalistic records from 1865 refer to the number of 'disguises' being more numerous than ever. 1857 gives a reference to details of a tableau which, having been in the procession, was subsequently thrown on the bonfire. So we can assume that in 1857 the tableaux were still wooden cut outs or stuffed dummies and not human as they are today!

Size restricitions

The evolution of the carnival was a slow process but twentieth century technology helped to speed it along. Tractors replaced horses and electrical generators replaced paraffin torches. The 'carts' became bigger and better. In 1934 one of the biggest floats to date was produced when *Skiers of St Moritz* appeared and was 55 feet in length. But more was to come and it was necessary to introduce a rule limiting the size of the entries to a maximum of 100 feet long, 11 feet wide and 17' 6" high. Despite those official restrictions, clubs were prepared to push the limits, even to break the rules. I can remember when I was involved in float building, we always knew when the man from the committee would be coming to measure our float. We also knew that he never measured the height and it was easy to pull the wool over his eyes in respect of

Swayne's Shoes of Bridgwater. Charlie Swayne was for many years a member of the Bridgwater Carnival Committee.

the length. The width we could not get away with. He would come with his tape measure, and with an assistant, measure the width of the cart in the middle, but not at the front or the end. He would then measure the length of the cart and the generator trailer, but not the tow bar which connected the two and he would forget the tractor.

Was it any wonder that floats entered the procession over length? By 1988, a more thorough regime had been introduced and the Cavaliers Carnival Club were only allowed to enter the procession at Bridgwater after they removed their name plate from the front of their entry which brought the length to just inside the limit. Another club swapped its tractor tow bar for a shorter one. In 1989, the police stepped in at Wells Carnival when, prior to the procession, they measured the lengths of the entries. Many of them were over length. The very first one they measured, a Bridgwater club, was a 117 feet long. All the floats over length were withdrawn from the procession. There was considerably bad feeling from the Wells committee who, perhaps justifiably, felt that the problem should have been ironed out at the first carnival, not the fifth. In subsequent years, the floats were measured by the committee officials as they entered the line up zone at Bridgwater Carnival. Nowadays, VSOs (Vehicle Special Orders) are required. These are applied for on an annual basis and, when granted, approve the passage of a carnival float on the public highway.

Back to the evolution of carnival. After the introduction of tractors and generators, the next development came with the generators becoming disguised as part of the entry, followed by the tractors such that the whole moving exhibit formed one complete illusion of the portrayal.

Official organisation

After three centuries of spontaneous carnivals, the event officially became organised in 1881. It was however still a relatively small procession by today's standards. By 1900 it had grown and contained many trade entries, the likes of which are not permitted today since neither space allows nor would they add anything to the spectacle other than to lengthen an already long procession.

In those days, and indeed well into the middle of the twentieth century, the procession lined up in the St John Street area and along the railway station into Wellington Road. The sheer number of trade exhibits is well demonstrated in the words of the following poem which was penned by A. J. Whitby and published in the *Bridgwater Independent* on 10 November, 1888. It is reproduced in full since it gives a wonderful insight into the nature, size and content of a procession from more than one and a quarter centuries ago.

The Bridgwater Guy Fawke's Carnival – (A long way after Macaulay)

Attend all ye who list to hear our carnival's delight,
I tell of the thrice famous larks we had on Monday night,[1]
When our Bridgwater Fireworks eclipsed in size again
The biggest blaze of Brock and Co., the stoutest squibs of Pain.[2]

It was about the lovely close of a bright November day,
There ran the troop of small boys round, exulting in their play,
For they had seen the Bonfire Boys at their congenial task,
From earliest twilight, on Cornhill come heaving many a cask;

And they escaped the school board man[3], and hung about the place,
And round the pile of wood enjoyed the pleasures of the chase.
For all day long the Bonfire Boys were gathering fuel galore,
All day from yard to yard they drove[4], they drove from door to door.

Till sixty barrels filled the space within the market gates,
Till packing cases towered aloft, with faggots, logs and crates;
And opposite the market house behold an iron-railed space,
Wherein behoves them to set up the bonfire in its place.

The fisher lent his skiff[5] to light the Saturnalian sports,
The ragged urchins roared around, from West streets sunless courts[6].
The sun was shining joyously, and all along the line,
'We're going to have it fine,' they said, 'We're going to have it fine!'

The freshening breeze of eve blew up, the afternoon grew cold,
The parting gleam of sunshine kissed those railings tipped with gold.
Forthwith a sail at every shop was placed along the street,
And firemen played with hose and jet to wet each flowing sheet.

Many a light errand-boy put out to pry along the way;
As fast from every village round they came to join the fray.
Night sank upon the noisy streets, and on the gathering spree,
Such night Bridgwater oft has seen and oft again shall see!

From Eastover to Taunton Road, from North Street to the Quay,
That time of slumber was as bright and busy as the day,
A 'bobby' pacing Wembdon Hill looked forth into the night,
And saw' o'er hanging Clarence roof a blood red streak of light.

---

[1]The reference to Monday night reflects the long standing practice of holding the carnival on 5 November. In 1888 it was on a Monday.
[2]Brock and Pain have long been two of the largest manufacturers of fireworks in the UK. Increasingly these days, fireworks are imported from abroad.
[3]The school board man's responsibility was to ensure as few pupils as possible played truant. This was particularly problematic at harvest time and carnival time.
[4]This is almost certainly a reference to the many brickyards around the town.
[5]A skiff is a light rowing boat for one person.
[6]Prior to redevelopment, West Street was lined with long terraces of cottages. Every so often, an alleyway between houses would lead to a courtyard at the back of the street around which would be clustered small and dark dwellings. These were pulled down as part of a programme of slum clearance.

'Twas four fair maidens caused the blaze on Cornhill's open space,
Till broad and fierce the flames came forth and raged and roared apace.
At once beside the station gates arose the answering fire,
At once the tradesmen's trophies splashed along St John's Street mire[7],

And east and west and up and down the fiery message flies,
To rouse in many an ancient pub, the chattering groups of guys.
Now from the farthest wards was heard the rush of hurrying feet,
All making for the station yard, where all the guys must meet.

The hobbler[8] left his skiff to rock on Parrett's slimy banks,
The brickies left their toil to join the great procession ranks.
We look down Eastover and see, while shouts rise higher and higher,
Torch beyond torch, in endless range, those twinkling points of fire.

With his grey charger well in hand, General Boulanger[9] comes,
Behind him march the fire brigade, Behind them sound the drums,
And lustily the Christies[10] play, and gaily dance the belles,
As slowly up the street there rolls a carriage-load of swells.

Look how the effigy of Fawkes lifts up his ancient head,
As underneath him steadily his stalwart bearers tread.
So glared he, when at Westminster in wrath he turned to bay,
Where in the cellar of the House, the powder barrels lay.

How gallantly the jockeys ride, and how the people stare
As streams in crimson on the wind the Chinese lanterns glare.
The admiral and sailor boys march on with swinging pace,
And the *Orlando* all the way has held them close in chase.

Then bugle's note and rattling drum the stately ship succeed,
And torch in hand, in red and white, the soldier boys proceed.
Ho! Gunners, fire a loud salute, ho! Curate, wave your nose,
As high on horseback by the gun the dark Commandant *Rose*.

With his white wig unbonneted, a handsome courtier rides,
While by him sits a jester, with two foreigners besides.
And waving red along the route, the torchlight still appears,
High on the Mandarins it shines, it shines on Cavaliers;

It streams o'er knight and lady, o'er Negro, Turk, and clown,
As slow the gay procession sweeps along the roaring town.
And all the different industries are represented here,
And as they pass the wondering crowd send up an answering cheer.

---

[7]Until 1924 there was no Tarmac or concrete road construction. By November, St John Street and other roads would be muddy and rutted.
[8]A dock worker who assisted in the mooring of ships.
[9]General Boulanger was a French military leader and an ardent nationalist. He was exiled in 1889 under suspicion of plotting a coup in order to become the dictator of France.
[10]Christies were the local silver band.

The 'Little Brown Jug' rides aloft, the potter's wheel spins round,
And Thompson's[11] tin pots clatter loud, Sparks fly, and knives are ground.
And see Symon's, Major's, and Barham's bricks and tiles[12]
Are being manufactured here in all the latest styles.

So work they when at Salmon Lane, or by the Castle Field,
They turn to brick the native clay the local claypits yield,
Look how the car of Culverwell lifts up its massive cogs,
While underneath the engineers stand in their working togs,

Ho! Sling thy type, compositors; ho! Small boy, roll the form,
For here the gallant printer lads their noble art perform;
Here Smith the saddler tells us all that 'nothing is like leather';
Here boiler-makers banging loud, work with good *Wills*[13] together;

And wood is carved , and marble chipped, and lathes are rent asunder,
While Carver's[14] shipwrights in their craft make all the craftsmen wonder.
The carriage sheds have sent a dray, with forge in fiery blast,
And Cresser's valiant fire brigade brings up the rear at last.

And on and on, with many a pause, they rolled from street to street,
And through Northfield and round the Square the drums were heard to beat.
Then far and wide from bright Cornhill the gangs of guys dispersed,
And rockets soared, and crackers banged, and squibs careered and burst.

And when we speak of squibs, you know, we mean them hot and strong,
Two inches in the bore, about eighteen inches long.
Once from the battery of one gun the Roman Candles poured,
From H.M.S. *Orlando* quick an answering broadside roared,

And all the Naval Volunteers charged with a louder cheer,
The gun was won, with lots of fun, the gunners fled in fear!
Now swift to east and swift to west the masqueraders ran,
To squib the folks around, who try to dodge them all they can.

And broader still became the blaze, and louder still the din,
As folks from every village round enjoy the fun and grin.
The Christies tunefully discourse beneath the market dome,
Until eleven, but not till two do all the crowds go home.

The carnival has ended now, in S - M - O - K – E
And when they have another one, may we be there to see.

[11]Thompson are the ironmongers and survive today as one of Bridgwater's longest established businesses.
[12]Symon's, Major's and Barham's were three of the leading brick and tile works based in the town.
[13]Wills Engineering were based on the Salmon Parade. They had their own carnival club which survives today still carrying the name of Wills.
[14]Carver's Yard was a shipbuilding business with its own dry dock on the East Quay. It was here that the last ship built in Bridgwater, the *Irene*, was launched in 1907.

George Burge with the last pair of horses to draw a carnival cart.

Edward VII's coronation year of 1902 was particularly successful as this theme encouraged a record number of entries. As in previous years, these were all horse drawn using pairs of shire horses which were decorated to fit the occasion. Each horse had well polished collars with hanging brasses and bells which jingled as they moved. Shining harnesses, brilliantly polished hooves and coloured ribbons added to the charm and appearance. Special prizes were awarded for these magnificent animals. The local Bown family were particularly known for their splendid turn outs. It was as late as 1948 that the last horse drawn entry appeared in the procession. It was the Crown Inn's *Yankee Doodle Dandies* with Mr. T. G. Burge taking the honour of the last driver of a horse drawn float. It was my wife's uncle, Albert England, who had the responsibility for bedecking the horses with their illuminations.

Carnival under threat

It was in 1913 that the first entry appeared with battery powered illuminations and this proved to be perhaps the most dramatic turning point in the evolution of carnival. However, it wasn't all good news that year. Chief Constable W. J. Davey was newly appointed to the town and, being from Wales, lacked any understanding of local culture and traditions. He had received a letter from the Home Office asking if it was true that there was to be a bonfire in the town with giant fireworks being discharged. Davey felt it was his duty to cancel the event. Thousands congregated outside of the *Bridgwater Mercury* office to await an announcement. The council met in emergency session, but the best they could propose was to move the carnival procession to the playing fields in Cranleigh Gardens. The idea was not well received and the crowd made their feeling obvious.

Davey was adamant. If the committee continued with the organisation of the event, then arrests would be made. The committee took legal advice and eventually found a solution. They knew that with or without officialdom, the carnival was going to happen anyway. The crowd outside the Mercury office raised a cheer when the committee published their announcement. They had written to the Chief Constable stating their disassociation with the event that was going to take place. A notice went up in the window of the *Mercury* office stating that the carnival procession which WILL NOT be organised this year WILL leave the railway station at the usual time! In other words, people power had prevailed with or without the committee's support or Davey's interference.

The lead article in the following week's *Mercury* referred to the 'thousands of excursionists who visit Bridgwater every year to witness the carnival bear testimony to the admirable manner in which it is now organised and controlled, and the exceedingly good humour prevailing. It is generally hoped, therefore that the seemingly uncalled for endeavour to prevent its continuance will prove unavailing'.

How true those words are even today! This was somewhat reminiscent of our local police chief's involvement some eighty years later when the message in the local papers was along the lines of 'shift it or lose it!'. It was another case of history repeating itself thanks to a total lack of appreciation of local culture. After the 1913 incident, any goodwill between the local population and the borough police force rapidly evaporated. But also of interest in that report is the reference to the thousands of excursionists who flocked to the town. As we will see later, this created a problem for the other Somerset towns where there were insufficient people left to support their own towns' events.

The advent of electricity

Traditionally the procession had always been lit with paraffin torches. Then came battery power followed by the advent of generators. The impact of these cannot be overstated. Today generators of half or even a full megawatt are the norm, powering perhaps 20,000 lamps and numerous motors. There was a time when the cold nights of November cut to the very marrow of the performers on their floats. Some themes justified scantily clad maidens as part of the entry and these in particular were prone to the chilling effects of the winter winds. Often these young girls would be taken off the floats in an almost hypothermic state. The powerful generators of today have significantly reduced that problem. With eighty percent of the energy in each light bulb being given off as heat, the lighting now

Above: *Performer from Wills Carnival Club's* Lore Ring of the Magnaki *benefits from the heat given off by the lighting. The picture below shows how early lighting produced outlines.*

creates a warm area in which to perform irrespective of the weather.

1903 was the milestone year when electricity first appeared in a procession. The Newton Electrical Works of Taunton produced *The Blue Bell Minstrels*, a float illuminated by electric current. Ninety incandescent light bulbs were powered by a dynamo attached to an engine mounted on their float. The world had never before experienced such a display and the crowd gasped in amazement and wondered where it would all end!

The earliest popular use of generators involved power supplies measured in kilowatts, perhaps 25 or 50 kilowatts, and eventually 75 kilowatts. Such low powered generators only permitted a limited number of bulbs to illuminate the entries. The earlier floats on which these were used had no roofing, no ceiling from which light could be thrown down onto the performance. Hence the greater part of the light bulbs would run around the perimeter of the deck of the entry. This meant that a large number of light bulbs were exposed to the elements and pointing upwards. Any rain water was liable to run down inside the bulb holders, so rubber seals were used, and if it was a cold night,

just a single drop of rain landing on a hot bulb was sufficient for it to explode. Hence most of these lights out of necessity were of low wattage. As the power of generators progressed, so the lighting was used to outline the shape of the main parts of the portrayal, for example the outline of a ship.

The introduction of roofs and white ceilings took the whole presentation forward with higher wattages being used and capable of illumination from above. As the power of the generators grew, there was no looking back.

Of course, generators can bring their own problems. If the power fails, the club loses all of its lighting and there is no more soul destroying sight than a carnival float in procession with no lighting. Audiences are always generous in their support for such entries, with larger than normal applause to encourage the performers along. In the event of the power being restored, it is always greeted with a huge cheer from the spectators and members alike. Generators can also catch fire. In 2003 the young performers of the Key Kids Carnival Club from Meare were evacuated from their float at one of the carnivals and the procession held up while firemen dealt with the fire.

YMCA take delivery of a generator

Carnival Cavaliers complete with swords and squib coshes.

Development of themes

Looking at old carnival photographs from across the last century and at written reports from the nineteenth century, it is easy to see how a change in choice of themes has developed. From the early days of guys and fancy dress, the carnival evolved to include trade exhibits. These reflected local industry and were phased out as the number of true carnival entries grew. During the first half of the twentieth century there were two world wars. There was also less money available compared to today. Overwhelmingly during those years, the majority of the carnival fraternity would have worn a uniform at some stage in their lives, whether they had been called up to fight in the wars or whether they were amongst those conscripts during the years of national service. Hence, when it came to tableaux in particular, those entries which portray an unmoving scene, there was a natural inclination to choose themes of a military nature or depicting royalty, where standing to attention for long periods was appropriate behaviour. Hence these themes predominated.

The *Bridgwater Mercury* for November 1886 describes how one club portrayed *Pictures from the Pack* based on the contents of a pack of cards. Being a tableau they portrayed four scenes, Sunshine, Cloud, Storm and Calm. Sunshine was portayed with four Jacks sat at a table playing whist whilst others watched on. In Cloud, the Jack of Diamonds, having thrown down his cards, challenges the Jack of Hearts who stood accused of cheating. The other two Kings tried to restore calm to the angry situation. In Storm, furniture was overturned and the two Jacks, unable to agree, were fighting a duel with swords. The Kings of Diamonds and Hearts acted as seconds. The tableau ended with Calm. The Jack of Hearts lay mortally wounded in the arms of the Jack of Clubs. Whilst the Ace of Hearts checked the victim's pulse, the King and Queen of Hearts wept at his feet. A satisfied Jack of Diamonds wiped his bloodied sword. It was Victorian melodrama at its best and received rapturous applause as the curtain folded on the scene.

Knights provided a more romantic military theme.

Devonshire Arms continue the military theme.

Political correctness

But this left the features, those singing and dancing entries, still to choose their themes for the season. The problem many faced was that whilst their members were keen on carnival, they perhaps lacked a degree of confidence when it came to performing in front of a crowd. And so their themes were frequently chosen because of the 'disguise' which they required. Thus going for an African tribe, Zulus perhaps, allowed the individuals to hide behind black make up. Today political correctness and attitudes towards race are entirely different and themes where the members need to black themselves up are rarely seen. You may get blue make up for Ice Warriors, perhaps green for Martians, but not black for African tribes. Red Indians are a popular modern day theme with their war paint, but no longer will you find entries with such offensive titles as 'Coons, Wogs and Niggers' which I quote as an actual entry which appeared in the carnival concerts during the 1880s. The

Dahomey Warriors, whose picture is shown, demonstrate well the use of make up as a disguise. This old photo from 1883 clearly shows the squibbing coshes which are distinctively unique to the Bridgwater carnival clubs.

Almost a hundred years later, clubs were still producing such entries. The following photo shows the Gremlins Carnival Club with their Black and White Minstrel theme, at one time even acceptable to the BBC, and still acceptable in 1992. But in 2003 when Wick Carnival Club produced their theme of *Alabama Bound*, there was a reaction from some quarters with the implication that the Council for Racial Equality may become involved. The carnival committees considered the issue and the club were allowed to take part with no alteration to their performance. Once again common sense had prevailed. However, only a few years earlier, a young lad appeared in the Bridgwater Carnival concerts performing songs by Al Jolson. Objections to his appearing with black make up were upheld and thereafter he performed as a white Al Jolson!

Gremlins Carnival Club black up for their minstrel show in 1992.

Dahomey Warriors with their Bridgwater squib coshes.

For both the features and the tableaux, the themes have moved on. Many now are based on West End shows or musicals, block busting films or the latest popular books. In recent years, when Disney has produced films such as *Hook*, *Aladdin* or *Beauty and the Beast*, it is quite predictable that there will be a significant number of entries in the procession portraying those themes. Of course, there are still the perennial favourites such as Pirates or Red Indians, Showbiz or Ice Warriors, Spanish or Irish. The opportunity to produce something truly original is now quite elusive. Almost everything has been done before unless someone writes a new best seller such as *Harry Potter*, and then so many clubs will choose that theme that the originality is lost amongst the preponderance of entries portraying the same topic.

And so the originality today comes more in the way in which an idea is presented than in the idea itself. The float designs are increasingly complex and the carpenters of yesteryear have been replaced with the engineers of today. Almost all of the major entries will actually be designed on computer systems using CAD software (computer aided design). This technology is essential where the most competitive features rely heavily on the spectacle of rapidly revolving illuminated elements of their entries. The floats also are now of such a size that they are not permitted onto the public highway without a VSO (Vehicle Special Order) which states that the vehicle is safe and roadworthy. It is something like an MOT for carnival floats.

Raw materials

Another recent change is in the choice of materials. The huge models often portrayed on these floats are no longer manufactured from papier-mâché which goes soggy and collapses with the first decent November deluge of rain. Today those models are more likely to have been produced using fibre glass or polystyrene blocks which can be glued together and moulded with a hot knife.

PART 4

Carnival Concerts

Unique to Bridgwater, just like the squibbing, are the Carnival Concerts which have been an integral part of the festivities for well over a hundred years. These concerts are performed by the Bridgwater clubs as part of their fund raising programme but these days the importance of the concerts as part of the overall competition has greater significance than the income they generate. The very first concert was held on Wednesday, 31 October 1883 in the Bridgwater Town Hall and was a sell out. Originally a fairly amateur affair, this annual fiesta has reached very high standards of theatrical entertainment, in many cases matching the highest professional standards of stage craft – but it wasn't always thus.

It all began with Bridgwater having a new town bridge. The old town bridge had served the town well, at least until the 1840s when the town docks opened on one side of the river and the railway arrived on the other. This brought with it a huge increase in horse drawn traffic across the bridge but the bridge was too steep for the larger loads. Hence a new bridge was built and was completed in October 1883. It was decided that the official opening would take advantage of the carnival procession to make it an even more notable affair. It was originally hoped that the bridge would be opened in the May of that year in time for the Bath and West Show which was held in the town, but unexpected delays had put completion well behind schedule.

The carnival committee decided that to do justice to the occasion, they would have a firework extravaganza with sky rockets, Roman candles and 300 blazing torches. But the money for this needed to be raised and it fell to the Bridgwater Amateur Christy's Band to come to the rescue. They organised a concert.

Ramblers stage show for 2003 Midnight Express.

The carnival procession passes over the newly opened bridge, 1883.

At that very first concert, the show opened with the Christy's Band performing. This was followed by Mr F. Shepherd singing *Dream Faces*, a duet by Humphreys and Staples singing *The Pilot Brave*, and Miss L. Austin performing *Won by a Rose*. Another fourteen various solos and duets completed the show which finished with Mr F. J. Squire, who was the show manager, and his comic song *The Unfortunate Man*. Not a single carnival club appears to have been performing unless those in the cast had been from the clubs themselves. It was clearly a complete contrast to the shows we can witness today. According to press reports, over 1200 people formed the nightly audience. There has to be some doubt over this unless they were packed in the Town Hall like sardines. In my early days in the carnival concerts, the audience was around six hundred. In more recent years this has been reduced to four hundred to cater for the stricter fire regulations. To pack 1200 in must have required a largely standing audience.

Meanwhile, back at the town bridge, there was an official opening to be completed. The mayor at the time was W. T. Holland and if you take a look at the plaque on the town bridge, it tells how he opened the bridge in 1883. But he didn't. It seems that on the day of the big occasion, he went down with a dose of gout and his wife stood in for him.

After cutting the ribbon, the official party processed up to the Town Hall for the celebratory feast, Madame Mayoress in a horse drawn carriage escorted by Bridgwater's own regiment, the West Somerset Yeomanry, and followed by the carnival procession. Mrs Holland, in her husband's absence, read his prepared speech and then excused herself declaring that she felt it her duty to be at her husband's bedside. According to local legend this took her husband by surprise. On arriving home, at the riverside house we know as *The Lions*, she allegedly found her husband in bed with one of the maid servants!

I earlier made reference to an entry in the 1880s entitled 'Coons, Wogs and Niggers'. The very title provides an impression that it was perhaps more important to put on a cheap show with little real effort than it was to produce a performance that was for the benefit of the public rather than the performers. Despite the obvious early amateur nature of the show, over the years the demand for seats grew and grew. In 1886, it was necessary to hold two performances and this was further increased to three in 1920. In 1938, they were extended to a week and by 1950, this popular show had extended to twelve nights. Right through into the 1960s, although fine performances could be experienced, in amongst them sub-standard performances similar to those mentioned earlier were still appearing on the stage. Even the front curtain acts were often of a very low standard, the sort of performance where a group of men donned tutus and appeared as incompetent ballerinas. It was also seen as an acceptable practice to appear on the stage in an inebriated state. Solo singers would appear and be completely incapable of hitting the right notes or remembering the words. The later it was in the evening, the worse the problem would be. Indeed, some members of the audience would leave as they approached the final hour rather than tolerate a poor performance. These acts did nothing for the audience and the need to improve the show was recognised.

Perhaps the single most effective change was the introduction of auditions for the front curtain acts. No longer could the performers of previous years assume that their places on stage were theirs as of right. At the auditions, the weaker acts would be weeded out, and along with them those acts who perhaps performed well at previous auditions but

let themselves down during the live performance of the previous year. More than one old stalwart of the stage met their theatrical demise this way. It was even considered to be better to have a blank curtain than a sub standard performance. Gradually the standards improved to the high standards of today. This improvement rubbed off on the clubs as they saw a more credible supporting cast being built around them.

Other improvements were taking place at the same time. The structure of the show is such that each Bridgwater club has its time slot on stage in which to compete. In between the appearance of any two clubs, a front curtain act would perform. This act provides the time within which the previously performing club can remove all of its stage scenery and props from the stage whilst the next club brings in and positions theirs. So typically a club will appear for eight minutes with the front curtain act taking five minutes. This all came under the control of the stage manager. However, there was a time when clubs would take longer than their

Marketeers entry Rock 2003.

allotted time, both whilst performing and whilst bringing on the stage props. It became common place for the show, which started around 7.00 p.m. to finish well beyond midnight.

The problem was soon resolved with a change of stage management. The incoming manager, John Farrance, declared that any clubs going beyond their allocated time slot would have the curtain pulled on them. Of course no one believed that he would actually do it – but he did. Clubs found themselves chopping at least one song from their performance and the show came back under control. The public could now predict the time the show would finish. Under John Farrance's wing was Malcolm Jones, popularly known as the Cointreau Kid, who inherited and continued the tradition of practical stage management.

Part of the problem back stage is the sheer volume of props and scenery to be shifted between different clubs. Typically each club will have its own backcloth, its own scenery (or flats) and other properties, rostrums, trees, et cetera. As one club performs on stage, another awaits outside of the back stage doors. The curtain drops, the audience applause and the compére introduces a front curtain act. As he does so, the club just finished is already whipping their scenery out of the back door as fast as they can to permit the next club to bring theirs in. This is no West End theatre back stage, no opportunity to wheel out on one side of the stage and wheel in from the other. Everything goes in and out through the single set of stage doors. During my time as a committee member of the carnival, we received visitors back stage from the West End. They could not believe the energy and precision with which these apparent amateurs dealt with what they saw as the impossible. Where it does get hard for those club members is when it pours down with rain whilst they wait their call outside the stage door!

Recent decades have seen considerable improvements in the stage performances. Choreographers first made an appearance in the 1960s and immediately the difference they made was obvious. Previously most performers utilised what was called the carnival two step – step forward

Back stage crew under the leadership of stage manager Malcolm Jones (standing, far left).

Julia McDonald's Dancers 2003.

one pace, then one to the right, one back and one to the left, repeated as long as it took to finish the number, perhaps changing direction to demonstrate a bit of flair. Nowadays we can see the full range of dance movements, significantly enhancing the enjoyment.

Advances have also been made in the provision of the supporting music. In my early days, it was not unusual for the band and performers to be completely out of synchronisation. I remember one occasion when the band master turned over two pages of music instead of one. He played one number whilst we sang another. From the audience point of view, we were a disaster, completely unable to sing along with the band! On another occasion, thanks to the pace at which the band played, an eight and a half minutes performance on the opening night became a six minute performance on the second and we all left the stage breathless. With synthesised music used these days, the performers can be more confident that each performance will be consistent with each other.

It is an amazing statistic that at each performance of the carnival concert performance, several hundred performers tread the boards each evening. With so many enthusiastic amateurs on stage, mistakes inevitably happen. In my own experiences, I have witnessed quite a few. In the first year of the Renegades Carnival Club, we produced an entry entitled the Rainmakers. Parts of our costumes were very tall hats, so tall we supported them with hand-held guy ropes. With their hands out to their sides, the hat wearers entered the stage between the side curtains, shuffling out sideways from the wings. On our first night, one hat wearer shuffled sideways onto the stage and stood poised behind the stage curtain. The music started for the front curtain act which preceded us and the opera singer's curtain went back to reveal Madame Butterfly stood alongside one of our club members. He had shuffled out behind the wrong curtain.

On another occasion, I was the number two pair of legs inside a Chinese dragon. My colleague in the number one spot had his head inside the

Sally Williams' Dancers 2003.

dragon's head where a small slit permitted him to see where we were going. Unfortunately during one performance the head slipped and he was unable to see through the misplaced slit. With fingers crossed he headed towards the wings to exit the stage. However, his sense of direction had failed him and from my number two position I saw the edge of the orchestra pit approaching just as he was about to lead us all into it. It was a close call but not as close as one member of the Vagabonds Carnival Club. He entered the stage as a scuba diver, complete with face mask, snorkel and flippers. Unfortunately his mask steamed up and, true to the character of the diver he portrayed, he stepped over the edge of the orchestra pit and dived into the kettle drum. He was lucky to survive without serious injury. The kettle drum was not so lucky!

In addition to the clubs and front curtain acts, there are the dancing troupes. They always put on an excellent performance thanks to the professionalism of the choreography. These dance troupes and the front curtain acts have produced some exceptionally talented performers over the years. An early example was Stan Bevan who in 1948 performed 'Bless this House' for the Vagabonds Carnival Club and later went on to perform for the Sadlers Wells Opera Company. Shirley Sands who sang in the 1950's became a cabaret artiste and TV star. Carol Waterman went on to join the professionals under her stage name of Carol Lee Scott and plays the title character in the TV series *Grotbags*.

A more recent example is Andrew Jeffreys who after a period working in the local Cellophane factory, headed for the West End where he now appears on a regular basis. Another success story is that of Steve Paling, son of Alan Paling a well known Rambler. Steve honed his skills in the carnival concerts and now performs in the West End. At the time of writing, he has embarked on a world tour with the West End show *Mama Mia* as both director and choreographer. Steve's early potential is shown below when he took part with the Julia McDonald's Dancers in 1992. Julia followed in her mother's footsteps as a teacher of dance and her daughter, Katie Roach, continues the tradition. Katie is shown immediately to the right of Steve Paling.

Such is the popularity of the carnival concerts that a queue can start two days before the box office opens and all tickets for the two week show are sold out in just a few hours. The concerts help to emphasise the Bridgwater tradition of the act of entertaining being just as important as being entertained. This becomes even more obvious when one considers that in these concerts six hundred performers each night entertain an audience of just four hundred. How many other events can boast more performers than audience even with a sell out show? But what a dramatic comparison to the first concert in 1883 which was staged for just two nights. The modern show now lasts for a full two weeks with a total audience in excess of five thousand.

Shirley Sands, popular recording artiste and star of cabarets, the BBC and Bridgwater Carnival.

Steve Paling with Julia McDonald's Dancers before progressing to the West End.

PART 5
Geographic spread of Winter Carnivals

Various carnivals were taking place across the county in the early twentieth century, but they were small affairs and bearing no resemblance to today's spectaculars. In the early 1950s even Bridgwater's procession visited villages such as Cannington and Spaxton, such was the diminutive nature of the floats of those days. Other present day carnival towns went for decades without a carnival. North Petherton is one such example with its carnival procession being revived in 1949 after a gap of fifty years. In 1952, by which time Cannington had dropped off the circuit, the carnivals on the affiliated circuit were as follows:

Tuesday	4 November	Spaxton
Thursday	6 November	Bridgwater
Saturday	8 November	North Petherton Minehead
Monday	10 November	Highbridge
Wednesday	12 November	Wells
Friday	14 November	Midsomer Norton
Saturday	15 November	Glastonbury

By 1954 Spaxton was off the circuit and that was the last year Minehead was included. By 1961, although Midsomer Norton still holds a carnival, it was off the county list of affiliated carnivals.

Of all these, only Bridgwater can boast the continuity that permits it to claim the town as 'The Home of Carnival'. This boast can often offend those who come from other towns in the county but nonetheless have the same commitment to carnival. It is fair to say that, none of the carnivals would be quite the spectacular events they are without the involvement of those clubs from the other towns and villages. Glastonbury and Wells, and even Midsomer Norton, can boast some of the most successful clubs on the circuit. It is no longer a foregone conclusion that the county cups will go to Bridgwater clubs.

The circuits

Carnival has thankfully spread from its Bridgwater origins across the county and now even into neighbouring counties. So many now are the carnivals that they begin in August and finish in mid November without a Saturday available as a respite for those who do the three circuits involved. First in the carnival calendar are the carnivals of the Wessex Circuit with Sturminster Newton in mid August, then Trowbridge, Mere, Frome, Shaftesbury, Gillingham, Castle Cary and Ansford taking them through to mid October with Warminster finishing the circuit. In parallel with this, down in East Devon, another circuit is running with Seaton, Colyton, Axminster, Sidmouth, Newton Poppleford and Exmouth. Then comes the South Somerset Federation with Wellington, Ilminster, Chard, Taunton and Yeovil Carnivals. But even after all of these, the biggest and the best has yet to come. It is the Somerset County Guy Fawkes Carnivals. These start at Bridgwater and then appear at North Petherton, Burnham-on-Sea, Shepton Mallet, Wells, Glastonbury and Weston-super-Mare. It is here, on the county circuit, that the largest and most spectacular floats make their first appearances. Many of the entries which took place in the earlier series will also join these huge parades. And a fantastic sight they are as they pass through the mediaeval streets of these old Somerset towns, streets which seem to trap the light and sounds generated from these colossal entries, creating an atmosphere unrivalled anywhere in the world.

It is worth looking at a table of the dates of the various carnivals because it clearly illustrates how the floats from three different minor circuits all become available at the same time to join the big boys at Bridgwater. All the dates shown are for 2004 and are Saturdays unless otherwise stated. In June, July and August, the South Devon Circuit takes place at Newton Abbot, South Brent, Ashburton, Chudleigh, Kingsbridge, Torbay, Teignmouth, Bovey Tracey, Ipplepen, Dawlish, Totnes and Harberton Ford. Then the East Devon and Somerset Circuits start.

Date in 2004	Wessex Circuit	East Devon	South Somerset	Independent
21 August	Sturminster Newton			
4 September		Seaton		
11 September	Trowbridge	Colyton		
18 September	Mere	Axminster		
25 September	Frome	Sidmouth	Wellington	
2 October	Shaftesbury	Newton Poppleford	Ilminster	
9 October	Gillingham	Exmouth	Chard	
16 October	Castle Cary and Ansford	Broadclyst	Taunton (East Devon clubs join in here)	
22 October		Honiton		Crewkerne
23 October		Ottery St Mary		Honiton
30 October	Warminster		Yeovil	

It can be seen how the entries from these carnivals are on occasions split across three processions on the same evening. Then comes the Somerset County Circuit when these and the clubs from the 'premiere leagues' can come together in the world's greatest all-electric road show.

Date in 2004	Somerset County	Independent
Friday 5 November	Bridgwater	
Saturday 6 November	North Petherton	
Monday 8 November	Burnham-on-Sea	
Wednesday 10 November	Shepton Mallet	
Thursday 11 November		Midsomer Norton
Friday 12 November	Wells	
Saturday 13 November	Glastonbury	
Monday 15 November	Weston-super-Mare	

For many, it is Bridgwater which is the most important carnival at which to succeed. It is here for the first time that the biggest clubs compete head to head. The largest single contingent, especially in the features class, comes from Bridgwater. Whilst they compete against each other in the local class, the non-Bridgwater clubs compete in the open class. Once the procession is over, the High Street holds a collective breath while the results are announced. These set the pace for the rest of the circuit. At North Petherton, with the exception of the limited number of local clubs, the competitors come head to head for the first time, Bridgwater and non-Bridgwater all together. After five more carnivals, the results across the circuit of seven are known and the county champions can be declared.

Points are awarded for the positions achieved at each procession. The combined points are then calculated and the club with the highest points is declared the overall county champion and winner of the Starkey Cup. That club could be either a feature or a tableau. The Midsomer Norton Cup is then awarded to the best feature club.

Glastonbury

It is difficult to put a finger on when carnivals started in Glastonbury. There are numerous references to bonfires and squibbing back as far as 1850. General opinion seems to date it from 1854. Certainly the practice of rolling blazing tar barrels down through the High Street is recorded during the 1840s and 1850s. In 1870, the *Central Somerset Gazette* included a letter from a reader who disguised his identity with the pen name 'A Lover of Law and Order'. It referred to the recent report of a government inspector who had been sent to Glastonbury to investigate the nuisance created on the Saturday night by the firing of squibs and other such items, thus exposing properties to the risk of fire. But there is no mention of a procession, which doesn't mean that there wasn't one – just that it isn't mentioned.

In 1875 there was no Guy being mentioned but there were once again tar barrels. The practice was for local men to race down through the High Street with their burning barrels. In 1880 there is a reference to a 'Firework Carnival' in Benedict Street School where admission was by ticket only. There the Avalonian's Band played and at nine o'clock they paraded through the town. At the top of the town a procession was formed which led down to the market place where fireworks were let off, a variety of squibs and crackers having already been used along the route. It seems this is unlikely to be a procession as we know it today, not so much a procession watched by spectators, rather a procession formed by spectators who followed the band to the central bonfire. That same year a blazing tar barrel was carried head high and left to burn away in the High Street. The practice of rolling tar barrels down through the High Street continued for many years. Of course in those days the roads were made of dirt and open sewers ran down the street.

At 11.00 p.m. the deputy chief constable brought the proceedings to an end with the announcement that no one would be prosecuted for anything that had happened thus far that evening. Presumably the implication was that they would be prosecuted for whatever happened from thereon. His carnival spirit earned him a hearty cheer from the gathered throng who quietly went home.

1891 brought a year of confusion. It was considered appropriate that the carnival procession should be properly organised and hence the Carnival Club was formed. The problem was that there was already a group who organised the bonfire, The Bonfire Boys. They were less formal than the Carnival Club but considered themselves quite capable of running the show. So in that year, there were two organising groups, each organising a street collection, a procession, bonfire et cetera. The two groups, known as the old firm and the new firm, were eventually to work more closely together. Nonetheless, the Carnival Club built their bonfire at the top of the town and the Bonfire Boys built theirs at the Cross and each had organised a procession. To avoid potential conflict, the two groups had been prevailed upon to adopt different routes. Several thousand spectators gathered from the surrounding villages. At seven o'clock that evening both fires were lit. Then the Bonfire Boys procession started, passing down the High Street towards the Cross. First came the torch bearers, then the Street Brass Band and the masqueraders. These included *The Prince of Clowns, Guy Fawkes* (at twenty feet high), *Buffalo Bill, Turks, Niggers, Zulus* and *Red Jackets* and many others. After passing through Northload, they returned to the Cross where the Carnival Club's procession was also just arriving. Two carnivals in one night. They've never done that in Bridgwater! The two groups passed each other with no sign of trouble and a sigh of relief was breathed. At the market place, later that evening, the Bonfire Boys put Guy Fawkes on trial. As in previous years, he was found guilty and consigned to the flames of the bonfire.

The Carnival Club's evening had started in Benedict Street where the costumes, in excess of a hundred, were judged. *John Bull*, a *Zulu, Robin Hood, Ring Clowns, Darkest African Minstrels, King Hal* and numerous others came under the scrutiny of the judges.

In 1900, the Glastonbury Bonfire Boys met at the Crown Hotel to decide how to celebrate that year. It appears that significant numbers of Glastonbury folk were visiting Bridgwater to witness the procession there. Certainly records show large groups from the towns and villages within striking distance of Bridgwater deserting their home town celebrations in favour of the Bridgwater parade. This created cause for concern and many other towns and villages had to consider whether or not they should attempt processions of their own. The decision at Glastonbury was to hold a bonfire and carnival on the Cross but no procession. There are some who consider that these references to 'no procession' provide the evidence that there must have been processions in previous years, otherwise why would there need to be a reference as to whether or not there should be a procession? However, it is far more likely that it is a reference to not holding a procession in contrast to what was happening elsewhere in the county, in particular Bridgwater. Had there been such processions previously in Glastonbury, there would almost certainly have been journalistic or photographic evidence somewhere in the archives. Within two years of that meeting at the Crown Hotel, the celebrations at Glastonbury were sadly described as so feeble as to have passed unobserved, not even a bonfire. In 1902 reference was made to the occasional explosion of a cracker or squib, the whole event passing almost unnoticed. The people of Glastonbury were going elsewhere.

By 1920 the local press still referred to Glastonbury Carnival as a 'has been' affair with an exodus of Glastonbury folk travelling to Bridgwater. There had, however, been a bonfire in Chilkwell Street and Hillhead for the benefit of the local children. It appears that during 1921 and 1922, a dozen or so carnival enthusiasts met in the Rifleman's Arms in Chilkwell Street and pulled together plans for a carnival. It proved to be the carnival which led to the one we see today and realistically it is from this point that we can trace the heritage of Glastonbury's spectacle. The 1923 parade could definitely boast a significant number of masqueraders and included the effigy of Guy Fawkes and a squibbing display. As at Bridgwater, the entries were illuminated with paraffin torches. Prize money and fireworks associated with the event necessitated a source of income and so the Glastonbury committee organised many events such as jumble sales, raffles, house to house collections, fetes, dances and even horse racing in the Abbey Park.

One entry in those early years sadly failed to complete the route. The club members had arrived at Fisher's Hill and decided to refresh themselves in the Globe Inn. Leaving their horses and cart outside the inn, they re-emerged later only to discover the horses had been stolen! The route in those days started at Chilkwell Street, then down the High Street, into Benedict Street, Fisher's Hill, Bere Lane and back to Chilkwell Street.

Decades later, in 1989 a campaign was held to get the Glastonbury Carnival extended all the way to the neighbouring town of Street. The original idea came from Glastonbury's deputy town mayor and was seen as a way to allow more people to watch the procession and to ease parking problems. But the Glastonbury Carnival Committee did not find the idea acceptable and common sense was allowed to prevail. For the performers it would have meant something like a four hour procession!

Although the carnival survives today with its unbroken tradition (war years excepted), it came close to finishing in 1963. However, there were those who were determined that the show must go on and in that year's carnival there were just two floats in the parade, the Carnival Queen and Bridgwater's Lime Kiln Carnival Club, who deserve our congratulations for their commitment and vision.

Wells

Meanwhile, in the nearby city of Wells, the first recorded carnival procession took place in 1902 and the proceeds from the collection totalled less than £1. By 1925, Wells was advertising prize money of £50 to entice masqueraders to their procession and both Glastonbury and Wells were now being visited by horse-drawn carnival carts arriving from the Bridgwater area.

Both Glastonbury and Wells Carnivals thrive today and are popular on the circuit. Their narrow streets create a warm and exciting atmosphere as the floats pass through and each of these venues also support a significant number of local clubs producing entries to the very highest standards. The streets of both towns are filled almost to capacity on the nights of their carnivals.

North Petherton

Records of Guy Fawkes celebrations in North Petherton go back to the late nineteenth century but with no early suggestion of a procession other than a journalistic reference to the 1949 revival of the procession being the first for fifty years. In all probability, that earlier procession would not have been a procession as we would recognise it today with spectators watching performers but, in similar fashion to Glastonbury, with the spectators themselves forming the procession, travelling along with masqueraders With the proximity to Bridgwater, it was unrealistic to expect a procession on a similar scale at such an early stage but the revival in 1949 saw no fewer than 72 entries with many of those from its carnival neighbour. The winner received the Clarence Cup, named after the Clarence Hotel, known today as the Walnut Tree Hotel.

By this time electricity was prevalent albeit paraffin torches were still present in minimal numbers. Such a sizeable entry was a tremendous success for this newly launched carnival. The 1950s saw a decline in the number of entries, dropping to just forty or fifty. The 1960's saw a revival and it has remained a well attended procession ever since, both in terms of entries and spectators. The logistics of holding such a large procession in North Petherton were undoubtedly made easier when the M5 motorway allowed the town to be by-passed. However a recent attempt to reverse the direction of the procession as it travels along its stretch of the A38 proved somewhat disastrous. After a one year trial, the idea was abandoned.

There is only one major local club of any strength associated with North Petherton, being the tableau club Pentathlon who have put on excellent entries over the years. The other major entries at North Petherton come from the other Somerset towns.

Highbridge and Burnham-on-Sea

In similar fashion, Burnham-on-Sea was a later arrival on the carnival circuit and one which was none too popular on a cold winter's night when a chill wind blew in off the sea as the procession passed along the sea front. Fortunately today the procession passes within the sheltered streets and the huge generators prevent the cases of hypothermia once experienced. One aspect of Burnham which lends itself to carnival celebrations is the beach and, in years gone by, this was a popular spot for the town's main bonfire. Today, sponsorship permitting, it remains the favoured location for an enormous firework display which is provided on the night before the grand parade.

A significant difference between Bridgwater and Burnham Carnivals is the presence of a Carnival Queen at the latter event. The carnival queens are used as a means to boost the money raised for the carnival. The young ladies who apply to be queen compete to see who can raise the most sponsorship. The winner is crowned queen for a year and takes part in the parade. At Bridgwater, of course, such a spot is the preserve of the Guy Fawkes tableau.

The Burnham Carnival actually began as a Highbridge event with the procession starting at Alston Road. So Highbridge had its one-night-a-year winter carnival and Burnham had its summer carnival, a week long affair with different activities every day. Eventually the two became one. In 1961, Highbridge was off the county circuit but was revived in 1967 as the Highbridge and Burnham-on-Sea carnival and has survived that way ever since.

Shepton Mallet

The origins of Shepton Mallet's carnival are somewhat unique. It all began because the town needed a community centre. In the early 1960s the Shepton Community Association was inaugurated to raise funds for the project. Organisations from across the town and surrounding villages pulled together and it was agreed that bringing carnival to Shepton was one way to draw in the much needed funds. A carnival committee was set up in 1965 and carnival came to Shepton Mallet. Over the following decades, thousands of pounds have been raised for local charities. Unfortunately donations to the community centre fund were stopped when it was realised that for various reasons the centre would not be set up. However, that meant a larger share for the other charities. Moira Kerslake was amongst those founder members and was still serving as secretary decades after. Her husband Bob has also been involved as trade stand convener. After thirty years of chairmanship Lionel Edwards handed over the chairmanship to Don Clifford who remains in place today.

Getting the carnival launched required money and the team pulled together to organise a 50-50 auction. Brian Seal, when later reporting on this

event, paid tribute to the commitment of the auctioneer, claiming that scratching his ear had landed him with a set of three vases. In the years that followed, the sponsorship raised by the carnival queens and princesses has done much to cover the running costs. Over the years the carnival grew and in 1978 there were a record 151 entries. It was at this stage that the decision was made to no longer plough money into the community centre fund, there still being no visible progress on that project. It was however the year which saw the first appearance of the Bambi Carnival Club, taking its name from the Bambi icon associated with Babycham, the sparkling drink produced locally by Showerings. Another new entry was the Fielders Carnival Club, a spin off from the Crown Inn, with their entry 'Terror of Orthoptera'.

In 1982, a European influence was felt as the Fireman's Band of Misburg, Shepton's German twin town, led the procession. The following year witnessed another German influx with a contingent from Hanover Prison lining the route – fortunately officers and not inmates, or so they said. Fielders returned after a year's break, and along with Bambi were the only local mounted entries. Frome's Chameleon Carnival Club took the honours with their splendid *England Expects*. Sadly by 1985, although the procession that year was one of the most spectacular, there was not a single local float, all the local entries being on foot. Part of the problem lay with difficulties the Fielders Carnival Club were experiencing in respect of their building ground. The following year they managed to bounce back and Bambi were to join them. In 1987 Fielders appeared in new clothing as the Shambles Carnival Club with *Martial Arts of the Orient* and remain excellent ambassadors for Shepton Mallet as a carnival town.

Weston-super-Mare

Completing the Somerset Circuit is Weston-super-Mare, which made its debut in 1969 as the newest of the county carnivals. Crowd sizes at Weston are noticeably smaller than at other carnivals which brings its own benefits. Parking can be readily found and at the end of the evening, getting away from the town is much easier than the other venues. If you arrive late at Bridgwater, you can expect to be at the back of a crowd which can be up to twelve, even twenty people deep. Not so at Weston. It is, however, a carnival which has had more than its share of unexpected incidents. In recent years there has been a fire in a fish and chip shop which held up the procession, and no sooner had that been sorted out than a generator caught fire on one of the floats. Another year saw a gas leak and perhaps the most memorable was the sniper! A young lad had gone onto a higher level of a multi-story car park and from there fired an air rifle into the crowd. Whilst life would be easier without these incidents, I have been able to take advantage of them. In delivering training courses for event stewards, I have used several case studies by way of examples of those unexpected incidents that a steward may have to deal with. Every case study comes from Weston-super-Mare!

The other circuits

Whilst Weston completes the 'Magnificent Seven', other circuits exist within and without the county. These include the Wessex Circuit and the South Somerset Federation. At one time, these other carnivals produced little to compete with the 'big boys' but over the years they have been closing the gap and whilst these other carnivals lack the numbers and size of floats of the bigger carnivals, some of their clubs on an individual basis are

producing worthy entries which can compete with pride alongside the best. The most recent example of this is South Somerset's Gemini Carnival Club from Ilminster which in 2004 took the overall county cup with *Pirates of the Caribbean*. Having completed their own circuits, many of the entries from these other circuits finish their season by attending Bridgwater Carnival at least, and many then go on to complete the rest of the major league circuit.

The success and continuity of these smaller carnivals is important to the future of carnival as a whole. The increasing focus on health and safety, the increasing cost of putting on a carnival and the ever growing pressures on the organisers can only serve to make it progressively more difficult to keep this season of carnivals going. And so, as one carnival organisation struggles for survival, another will be gaining in confidence and thus maintaining the continuity. As recently as 2002, Crewkerne joined the carnival circuit with a late October Friday carnival.

Courtesy: Mrs Ena Hawkins

The Maharaja of Jammu and his Personal Retinue *2nd place tableau. The Malt Shovel Inn Carnival Club 1933.*

PART 6
Carnival as an Art Form

It amazes me that South West Arts and similar bodies have never financially supported our Somerset carnivals. When I look at some of the ventures into which they have poured money, I view the results in disbelief. Projects supported appear to have little community involvement and with a limited number of individuals benefiting from the funding. Carnival on the other hand involves thousands of people in the artistic production of the carnival entries and all with no funding other than that which the clubs raise through their fund raising efforts and the limited amount of appearance money.

Despite this apparent lack of recognition, carnival is undoubtedly the biggest, most highly visible expression of art in the West of England. If carnival was performed in a theatre, perhaps there would be greater recognition from those who hold the purse strings. Perhaps they fail to recognise each float as a moving stage, a theatre in its own right, on which the players strut and fret their hours against a background of the most elaborate settings and bedecked in magnificent costumes.

Shown below is the stage setting of the Wills Carnival Club's portrayal of *Lore Rings of the Magnaki*.

Stage show – Lore Ring of the Magnaki *from the Wills Carnival Club.*

Compare this with the float entry in the following picture. There is a clear difference in the two settings albeit the same theme is portrayed. The problem with the stage is the limitation of the club's ability to move the scenery into and out of the Town Hall in a matter of a few minutes. With the float, no such limitations apply, only those of space. Thus the scenery used on stage has to be of a light and manageable nature.

Road presentation – Lore Ring of the Magnaki *from the Wills Carnival Club.*

Some themes require considerable imagination to successfully portray the scene. Once again choosing Wills Carnival Club, below we see the float for their entry of *Cats*.

This theme was based on the West End show which in turn was based on the poems of T. S. Eliot. It was a story of life on a rubbish tip, where the cats hang out. And that was how Wills portrayed their choice of theme. Looking at the elements of the float, there are empty tins and boxes, watched over by columns of street lights. A simple setting but very effectively produced.

These pictures from the Wills club demonstrate how the effective use of lighting, in particular ceiling lights, show the portrayal at its very best. This style of float build up and lighting particularly suits the tableau who perform their unmoving scenes. The opportunity for large parts of the float to be moving does not present itself for the tableau and hence it is even more critical that costumes and make up are close to perfection.

Notice in the individual shown from *Cats* the perfection of both costume and make up.

Also notice how in the other picture, whilst one lady performs as a cat, the tractor driver is similarly dressed so as not to spoil the illusion. Rather like a swan that glides gracefully along on the surface of the water whilst its legs are going like the clappers beneath, the tractor driver will remain as motionless

as is practical whilst his hands and lower arms, hidden from public view, carefully steer the float safely along the route. Whilst the ladies shown must not move, there is no penalty for movement from the driver, but even he wants to perfect the illusion as best he can.

These pictures also demonstrate the high standard of stage make up. The viewing public will be within a few feet of these performers. The make up has to be realistic. Hence high standards of prosthetics, i.e. facial or bodily enhancement to create an illusion of a different form, can now be seen within carnival. A close up of a performer from the *Lore Rings of the Magnaki* is shown. The facial scarring depicted on the apparently injured performer shows the highest level of illusion. It has to – when the performer is viewed from just a few feet away.

One classic example of creative prosthetics was when the Ramblers Carnival Club recently used Sugar Puffs and Rice Crispies glued to their faces to create an illusion of faces deformed by radiation.

The building of the actual floats, which used to be completed in the period of two and a half weeks, is now an all year round affair. The clubs of today in the main benefit from building inside permanent

The illusion of scarring in Wills Lore Ring of the Magnaki.

sheds with the advantages that a stable site brings. Hence, once the carnivals are over, the clubs begin the process of choosing next year's theme. Generally speaking, by January they will have decided what they will be doing in the coming November and the building starts from there. As much material as possible is salvaged from the old cart. Light bulbs, holders and cable are stored away. Timber and steel are recovered as best as possible. In my early days, it was standard practice to burn the old bits of timber in order to recover the nails, so short of money were we!

Today clubs are better financed and better organised and many of them are able to recycle most of their materials. On occasions they even recycle the giant models they make. Wills Carnival Club having produced the *Charge of the Light Brigade*, sold the models of the horses they produced and the club which bought them, having used them, sold them again.

Griffens are past masters at this, having twice used a giant Gameboy. The picture on the opposite page top shows the giant models of surfers used in their theme *Surfs Up,* and the picture below shows how they were re-used by Tango, a juvenile carnival club from Sidmouth. In similar fashion, take a look at the Masqueraders year 2000 entry shown later and compare it with Key Kids Juvenile Carnival Club's 2003 entry and you will see the giant Warner Brother cartoon characters re-appearing.

From February onwards, the building work gradually increases in tempo until it reaches a climax as the carnival time approaches. For most clubs by the summer months, or early autumn, the moving parts on the floats will be undergoing test runs. The engineers will have produced CAD draw-ings which will have demonstrated that all the moving parts will work without colliding in to each other. Meanwhile, those with an artistic flair will have added bits and the moment of truth arrives as the chain-driven motors set the parts in motion. For the larger floats, there can be scores of such motors and moving parts.

Feature clubs often produce models as well as moving parts. Generally speaking, one will be produced at the expense of the other. Genies, lions, horses, bears, statues, Buddhas and all kinds of models are produced to enormous scales. In years gone by, the models were produced by applying layers of papier maché over layers of chicken wire stretched over timber frameworks. One good night's gales could completely destroy weeks of work. Nowadays most models are made of fibreglass or polystyrene. The latter is generally manipulated by gluing giant blocks of polystyrene together to create a single block large enough to produce the required item. The polystyrene is then carved with red hot knives which cut through the blocks like butter. Once the finished form has been created, a layer of plaster is usually applied and if required a layer of fibreglass to give a hard wearing finish. Where several copies of the same model are required, a fibreglass mould will be created from the original.

Producing spectacular floats is not sufficient on its own. The performers must do justice to the theme. A float which looks no more than average in daylight can be brought to life by the members provided the choice of music and choreography draw the best from the total performance. Observing carnival floats, one can separate them into a number of categories. Perhaps the most obvious, apart from features and tableaux, would be

Griffens Carnival Club present Surfs Up…

…and Tango Carnival Club recycle the surfers!

those clubs with a depth of engineers and those without. In similar fashion, once the performers are on board, they can be separated into those with a competent choreographer and those without. Marketeers entry of *Rock 2003* is a prime example of a float brought to life by the quality of the choreography and energy of the performers.

Often this can be seen in much smaller entries. A classic example of the power of choreography was the Wilfs Carnival Club portrayal of the *Wilfs' Synchronised Swimmers* which required a large blue plastic sheet to be towed along the procession route as though representing a pool of water. Holes were cut into the sheet through which the 'swimmers' would appear in synchronised fashion, complete with nose pinchers, and then would descend together.

For these walking entries, choreography is just as important as for the larger mounted clubs. Simply donning a costume and walking the route is not enough. The performers first and foremost must entertain and play to the crowd. Lisa and Dave Arney, shown left, have been doing this for years around the carnival circuits. And just look at the wonderful costumes where Emma Kingston from Wincanton is performing as Anne Boleyn in an entry entitled *Have you seen Henry?*, young David Griffiths performs as *Hook* and another entrant has produced a quite stunning candle.

The Kingston family have been regular visitors to carnivals for years and have produced some most imaginative themes. *I'm Armless* shown below demonstrates admirably how the individual performer can still produce an attention grabbing entry. Look closely at the photo and between the thumb and middle finger there is faintly seen a light patch indicating the sole of the performers shoe, the black shoes and trousers virtually invisible and creating a wonderful illusion of an armless hand processing along the carnival route.

Lisa and Dave Arney.

Wincanton, 1993. Emma Kingston presents Have you seen Henry?; *David Griffiths as* Hook; *an unidentified Candle.*

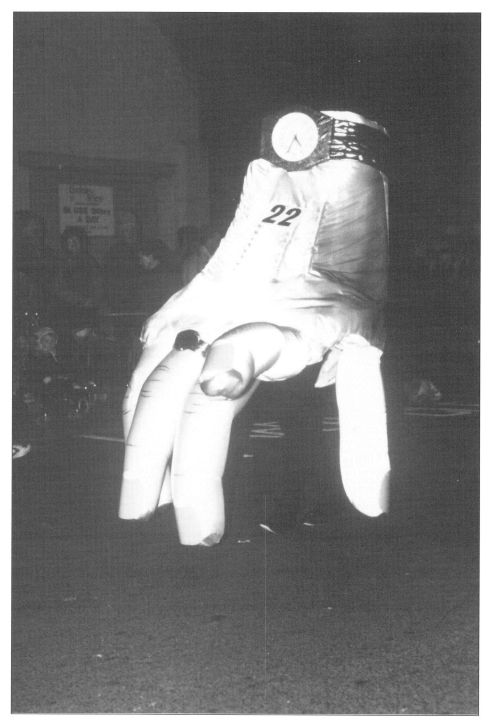

I'm Armless *by Bob Kingston of Wincanton, in 1995.*

PART 7
Fund Raising

It is not just the organisers of the carnivals who struggle to keep the show on the road. At club level, life is never easy. The sums of money involved in producing the huge illuminated floats, which are synonymous with the Somerset carnivals, are enormous. The costs are counted in the tens of thousands of pounds for each of the larger clubs.

In order to put its show on the road, a club has to raise the necessary finances. Fortunately, the club members provide all the labour involved free of charge, for the love of carnival. But materials for the floats and for costumes still need to be purchased. Insurance, which these days is astronomical, diesel for tractors and generators, which themselves have to be purchased or hired, coaches to take the clubs around the circuit; all these have to be paid for. And so there is a programme of fund raising which takes the club right through the year. Carnival is an all-year commitment for its members.

Since the costs are now so high, it is no longer sufficient to raise funds through low key ventures such as raffles or jumble sales. Far more commercial ventures have to be tackled. Cabaret nights, collecting glass bottles from local pubs for recycling, catering at weddings and outside events, providing event stewards at major public gatherings, sponsored walks, dances and discos, summer fêtes, member's subscription, the list goes on. The more successful the fund raising, generally speaking, the better the entry at the end of the year.

Marketeers provide an excellent example of what can be done with cabarets. They have had top quality acts in their cabarets, such as Ken Dodd, Faith Brown, Frank Carson and Paul Melba. Ramblers cabarets have tended to be more of the home-spun nature, or locally spun with top quality amateur acts occasionally supported by their own sketches. Numerous clubs now provide teams of stewards for major public events, in particular the world famous Glastonbury Music Festival. That major event required somewhere around 3000 stewards and a large contingent of these come from the carnival clubs. In order to ensure that the stewards are up to the job, they require certificates in event marshalling or event stewarding and these qualifications are on offer at Bridgwater College which has a team of people who are not only active carnivalites but who have professional training qualifications and between them offer a range of courses pitched directly at the carnival community.

In similar fashion, the college offers first aid training for event stewards and courses in food hygiene for those clubs who offer outside catering services as their fund raisers. Gremlins are a prime example and can be found each year at events such as *Yesterday's Farming* which is held annually in South Somerset. Numerous clubs around the county now recognise the popularity of quiz evenings, whilst others stick with old favourites such as bingo and raffles.

In addition to their own fund raising efforts, the clubs are assisted by the organising committees. Apart from prize and appearance money, which never reflects the real value of the entries, the committees will provide other opportunities. Bridgwater, for example, produce a carnival video and carnival calendars. Club members are able to sell these with the proceeds benefiting their own clubs. The sale of souvenirs has been a significant provider of funds and new ideas are always being tried. Souvenir badges prove popular and in recent

Robin Williams collecting at North Petherton.

57

years grand stand seats have been in great demand and more stands are introduced with each year.

Sponsorship is the one area where the committees actively seek support from local and national businesses but not so the clubs. The latter remain independent of the sponsors and perhaps it is best that they stay that way. Meanwhile, there is the collection and it has to be said that even in a record breaking year this can be disappointing with the average contribution per spectator being around 17p for two hours of entertainment!

So where does all the money go? It goes one of two ways. It either goes into the coffers of the carni-val clubs or into the funds of local charities. The charities are chosen each year and are then invited to supply collectors at the carnivals to go around the crowds rattling their tins. Basically the more they collect, the more can be handed over to their charity. Hundreds of thousands of pounds have been distributed to the various charities in this fashion. Often when discussing where the funds go, members of the public will comment that they are surprised that the clubs get a share. What they lose sight of is that each club is a charitable organisation in its own right, providing perhaps the most effective youth club in the South West.

Corsican Bandits from the Somerset Trading Co. Carnival Club of 1933.

PART 8

Introducing the Clubs

Carnival clubs consist of apparently ordinary people who become quite extraordinary in the carnival season. There is something in those who take part in carnivals which sets them apart. Enter a conversation with one and you'll realise that you're talking to a different breed. They show tremendous innovation and energy, discipline and talent, dedication and loyalty. It's not surprising that in times of recession, when unemployment runs high, carnivalites in general suffer less than most. The qualities which make them good carnivalites just happen to be those that make them an asset to any employer.

This willing band of volunteers put hundreds of hours into building the huge floats and into the rehearsals for their appearances on stage and road. Couple this with countless hours of fund raising as well as meetings, planning and organising the show, and you will soon realise that to be a carnivalite is an all year round, time-consuming and energy-channelling passion. Somerset can proudly boast the most active and effective youth organisation anywhere in the West of England.

Historically clubs were associated with specific local public houses and their names identified those associations. Throughout the twentieth century, certainly during the years of industrial prosperity, numerous clubs developed around the working environment. Labour forces formed tight knit communities, where individuals depended on the friendship of the others with whom they worked. Tight bonds were formed and so when a desire was felt to form a carnival club, it would often be developed in the workplace. This had the potential to offer benefits to the employer who could allow the workers to build their floats on the premises and through that further develop loyalty to the company as well as promoting the company's name as a caring employer.

In Bridgwater, examples of work based carnival clubs existed with Kraft (furnisher producers); Town Council employees; Hardy Spicer; Starkey, Knight and Ford (the local brewer); Hinkley Point Nuclear Power Station who became the Bohemians Carnival Club; British Cellophane; Coates Fencing; Quantock Preserving Company; Somerset Trading Co.; Wilkinson and Leng (Ironmonger); Wilmot and Breedon. The aptly named Splinter Carnival Club which appeared in 1949 were based at the Hooper's timber yard! Just one club survives today which in its name betrays its factory-based origins,

the Wills Carnival Club of Bridgwater. Wills was a local engineering company based in Salmon Parade which closed many years ago. The Wellworthy (piston manufacturers) Carnival Club survives as the Renegades. Outside of Bridgwater, the Bambi Carnival Club of Shepton Mallet has its links with Showerings and their Babycham product. Midsomer Norton has Prattens. Despite these, the majority of clubs begin and remain as clubs associated with public houses.

Whatever their origins, the future of carnival depends on the clubs, not only to provide the floats which create the overall spectacle, but to provide the future organisers. Every now and again, carnival needs a bit of nudge, and from such occasions come the rescuers, and often from one-and-the-same club. There was a post-war period of difficulty at Bridgwater when the members of the organising committee had been in place too long. A minor revolution took place when a number of ex-Vagabonds took over the reins. The carnival was soon to benefit from this injection of experience.

Amongst the members of the Kraft Carnival Club were Ken Gurd and Gordon Fisher. Ken was later to become the chief marshall of Bridgwater Carnival, with Gordon Fisher as his assistant. Ken oversaw the control of the procession during the years when many changes were taking place. Floats grew dramatically to the size we see them today and the number of entries grew significantly during the same period. The floats for Bridgwater Carnival, which once lined up in the roads around the railway station, outgrew the space available and the line up was moved to the Parkway dual carriageway at the east end of the town. The procession became so long that communication became impossible along its length without the introduction of two way radios. For many of the long-established marshals, the new technology was beyond their ability. Another injection of experience was required and another wave of ex-club members stepped to the fore.

From the Gremlins Carnival Club came a new chief marshall, Alan Jones, who saw the committee through perhaps the most difficult period of change with the police changing both their attitude and response to policing public events, in the wake of the Hillsborough football stadium disaster. Also from Gremlins came Bill King, Bridgwater's treasurer and his assistant Basel Patel. From Marketeers originally, and latterly from Wills, came both Rod

Stoodley, a long serving secretary to Bridgwater and publicity officer and now president, Chris Hocking. And so it goes on, with the clubs providing the spectacle and then sufficient of their experienced members, on retiring from club carnival, joining the band of organisers.

In looking at the clubs I begin with the largest single group, the feature clubs from the towns which form the Somerset County Circuit. These, along with their tableaux counterparts, are the big boys in the carnival league. These are the clubs which set the pace of change and the standards to be maintained. It is these clubs which with the tableaux compete for the county championship. The main prize is the Starkey Cup which goes to the club that gains the most points around the circuit and is competed for jointly by features and tableaux. The Midsomer Norton Cup is then awarded to the best club from the features and the North Petherton cup to the best tableau.

In 1886 a Bridgwater club presented Cards from the Pack. *Because of the bad weather and muddy roads, instead of walking they travelled in a Landau. The disappointed public were unable to see the fine costumes and so they re-appeared the following year.*

THE FEATURE CLUBS FROM THE COUNTY CIRCUIT

British Flag Carnival Club, Bridgwater

1992 British Flag's award-winning A Pirate's Life.

Historically there have been two British Flag Carnival Clubs, the former a tableau and the latter a feature. It was in 1938 that the pub first produced a tableau with its entry of *The Mounties*. It was a creditable beginning with the club taking second place on the road. Then the Second World War interfered and it was not until 1948 that the club was resurrected with *Merry Irishmen*, and another second place, The following years brought a run of second and thirds until in 1955 *Marco Polo* took top honours. Then came their final entry with the *Scene from Othello* taking third place. During their short history, three times they took first place as the best tableau in the carnival concerts.

Meanwhile, elsewhere in the town, the Roberts Brothers Carnival Club had been formed and it is this club which is the predecessor of the British Flag we know today. The Roberts Brothers first appeared in 1950 with *Gay Gondoliers*. That entry

brought them fourth place and in the years that followed similar results were achieved until in 1957 the club finally tasted success on the stage. First place was gained with *A Christmas Fantasy*, a success which was repeated the following year with *Bustles and Boaters*. The club was now appearing under its new name of the Revellers Carnival Club. Meanwhile the same two shows both achieved third place on the road and the club were optimistic for 1959. Their optimism was well justified when *Revellers of Bimbombey* took first on the road and second on the stage. 1961 brought them first place honours once again with *The Return of King Kong*.

It was in 1965 that they changed their name and for the first time appeared as the British Flag Carnival Club with a feature entitled *The Tommies*, earning fourth on road and seventh on stage. *Homer's Greek* and *In Old China* followed with both achieving second places. The club was clearly

SOMERSET CARNIVALS – A CELEBRATION OF FOUR HUNDRED YEARS

knocking once more on the door of success which came the following year when the *Kingdom of the Lost World* took the top spot on the road. 1969 to 1983 produced a string of excellent floats but which could only feature as also rans. Then in 1984 *Mexican River Festival* took them back to the number one position.

It was another six years before those heights were reached again when in 1990 they produced the most memorable *A Pirate's Life*. This wonderful float depicted a pirate ship which was brought to life by the enthusiasm of the members performing their

portrayals as those robbers of the high seas. Swashbuckling at the front of the float was the carnival stalwart Andrew Higgins. It was not just the float that made this entry so memorable. It was especially the music, *Victory*, and the way the members rose to the occasion. It was, in short, a classic and thoroughly deserved to be recognised as the best feature float in the county awards for that year.

Recent years have seen a bit of a drought in the trophy cabinet but the Flag remains one of Bridgwater's premiere clubs.

2003 Flag-A-Float.

Cavaliers Carnival Club, Bridgwater

There is something about the Newmarket Inn that attracts extroverts. Few pubs indeed can boast three carnival clubs. The first of these is the Newmarket Carnival Club itself, a successful comic feature club. Next is the Wilfs, also a comic club but on foot. Then comes the Cavaliers Carnival Club, one of Bridgwater's longest established clubs. Its origins date back to 1937 with the Coronoddies Carnival Club. Sidney 'Bungy' Thorne (who just happened to be my uncle), was a member of the Lime Kiln Carnival Club. As the result of a disagreement between club members, Bungy formed a breakaway group, the Coronoddies. The origin of this title is debatable. One opinion is that the club were based at the Coronation Inn in Bridgwater but as yet I have been unable to uncover the existence of such an inn. Another possibility, and the one which I prefer, is that the club took their name from the Coronation Year of 1937, the event being such a huge occasion. Initially they were still based at the Lime Kiln Inn.

Whatever the explanation, after two years war broke out and when the club reconvened at the end of the hostilities, they were based at the Golden Lion Inn in Bridgwater's St John Street and took the name of that pub for their 1946 entry of *The Caucasians*. It was a representation of the Cossacks, earning themselves fourth place at Bridgwater. Varying results followed, ranging from second to eighth until in 1951 they took first place in the carnival concerts with their *British Cavalcade*. In 1955 they hit the big time, their one and only moment of ultimate glory, with *The Ancient Egyptians* taking first place honours in the procession. This not only took the Kerr Cup for best in procession, plus the Hardy Spicer Championship Cup (combined stage and road results) but also the county's Starkey Cup as the overall county champions. They could now boast that they had won every major prize available.

Cavaliers 2003 entry of Voodoo.

The Golden Lion were always popular amongst the other clubs, not least because of such characters as Bill Granfield, Ern Pitman, John 'Fargo' Baker and my uncle, Sid 'Bungy' Thorne.

Fargo Baker was one of carnival's best loved characters, always ready to lend a hand, a word of advice and always offered with a smile. Bungy is probably best remembered for how long he continued to appear on stage, indeed well beyond retirement age. And then there was Ern Pitman. Ern was memorable for his wild behaviour whilst under the influence of cider. On a quiet night, he would simply tap on our front room window as he wended his way home, quietly saying 'Good night, Rog. Good night, Lorna'. This would set off our dog and who could blame him since this was usually between one and two in the morning. At his worse, he could be a danger, if not to others, then to himself. On one occasion he almost died when he accidentally swallowed the false beard he was wearing

In time, Ern and Fargo broke away to form the Golden Lion Old Boys who performed many a memorable front curtain act on the Town Hall stage during the carnival concerts, memorable usually because of Ern's inability to get it right.

Another stalwart from those Golden Lion years is Ivor Treeby. In 1980, the Golden Lion Carnival Club went through a metamorphosis and emerged as two. Whilst some members went to the Newmarket Hotel to become the comic feature club which is still based there, the remainder went to the Crown Inn just along the road in St John Street to become the Crown Cavaliers Carnival Club. In 1996, the club moved once again, dropping the 'Crown' from their title, and rejoining old friends at the Newmarket Hotel. The current club president is Ivor Treeby who provides that important link with the original club.

Today's club has failed to reach the dizzy heights of its 1955 predecessor but remains a popular member of the carnival scene. Despite its pedigree, it is still basically a young club and that youthful energy is much reflected especially in its stage shows. Their 2003 entry of *Voodoo* and 2004's *It's a Great Big Universe* both came seventh at Bridgwater.

Cobra Carnival Club, Wells

Life began in 1992 for the Cobra Carnival Club when it was formed at the Britannia Inn in Wells. Their first entry was as a non-comic feature entitled *Fire*. Amongst the founder members and still active in the club were Vince Graham and Paul Addicott. This relatively young club left the Britannia and moved to the Fountain Inn before their last move which took them to the Sports and Buses Club at Wells. In 1996 they tried a different discipline and appeared as a tableau entitled *Mortal Combat*. Perhaps after the seriousness of a tableau, they needed to refresh themselves the following year.

They entered as a comic feature with the *Hillbilly Smurfs*. It proved quite successful and brought home two second and two fourth places. Recent presentations, in which they have returned to the feature classes, have included *Heart of Christmas* in 2000, *Spanish Fiesta* in 2001, which they were still painting at 4.00 a.m. on the day of Bridgwater Carnival, and *Pinball Wizard* in 2002. This latter entry was perhaps their most memorable year with all members enjoying the pleasure of taking part with a worthy entry. Their 2003 and 2004 entries were *Dance of the Tribes* and *Caliente*.

Cobra presented Dances with Tribes *in 2003.*

Crusaders Carnival Club, Bridgwater

The Crusaders began life as the Hope Inn Carnival Club based at Bridgwater's Hope Inn and are arguably the longest surviving club in carnival. Their first entry in 1935 was *Revellers in Old Seville* which gave them early success with second place in Bridgwater. *Bavarians on Holiday* and *Clowns in Clover* were awarded 2nd and 3rd respectively in the following two years and then in 1938 came *The Jockeys* which brought them first place and the Bryer Cup, an achievement yet to repeated by this long established club.

The next six years were blighted by the war and it was in 1946 that they reappeared with all the other clubs. Their first post war entry was *Yukon Nights* and 1948 brought the *Cotton Pickers*. As can be imagined, it was not an entry that would do much on the road but was good enough to take first place on the stage, another result which has yet to be repeated.

There then followed a string of successful appearances which kept them in the frame but never quite reaching that number one spot. During the early 1950s my mother was their dressmaker and I well remember the intrigue each year surrounding the chosen themes. Even as a four year-old, I was sworn to secrecy. Among the most memorable entries for me were the 1953 *Alice in Wonderland*, memorable partly because of the range of costumes that the theme covered, with Alice, Mad Hatters, et cetera. But it was also because of the frustration experienced by my mother who, during every night of the carnival concerts, would have to sew the White Rabbit's tail back on, Arnold Sendell being unable to adequately defend his rear end.

The following year was *At the Races*, depicting a day at the races and it was the year I made my first appearance with the club. At just seven years old, I was a depiction of the famous flat jockey, Lester Piggott, the boy wonder of the day. Performing both on stage and road, I guess I remain one of the youngest carnivalites to complete the full circuit with a major club. As Lester Piggott, needless to say,

A Day at the Races *1954 – the author is the young seven-year-old boy in the centre.*

2002 Crusaders present the Aztecs.

I was on the winning horse at the front of the cart. However, all was not a bed of roses. The horses on which we sat during the procession were timber cut outs, about an inch thick with a narrow wooden saddle. They were good enough to take third place in Bridgwater but on arriving at Glastonbury, the organisers dropped a bombshell. They declared that we could not possibly enter as a feature since it was impossible to sing and dance when seated on a horse. And so we completed the route as a tableau, with me at seven years old remaining absolutely still for the hour and a half of the procession. Imagine the praise that was showered on me from the adult members of the club at the end of the evening. And, if I remember correctly, we even came away with a top place prize. Another memorable character from that entry was Stan Hamblin who portrayed the tipster Prince Monalulu, a colourful and famous, race-course tipster from the 1950s.

It was a float worthy of comment for another reason. It was the first time that a club had entered with a double trailer, that is a tractor, two trailers and a generator. In total it measured just over 120 feet in length, at least 20 feet longer than today's permitted limit. In those days, the procession route

in Bridgwater went through the relatively narrow Northfields with tight turns at each end. So skilful was the driver with the three trailers that he took both entrance and exit in one sweep without a pause to adjust or reconsider. Meanwhile, other clubs with just a single trailer were obliged to uncouple and manhandle their entries around the junctions.

1956 brought the *Red Devils*, with tridents and forked tails. This brought second place on the road, a result repeated in 1965 with *Invitation to the Ball* and in 1974 with *Horsemen of the Pegasus*. One controversial year was 1960 with the entry of *Ku Klux Clan*. It was the first time my mother contemplated not doing the carnival costumes. There was no way she wanted to associate herself with such a theme. It proved to be a generally unpopular idea and the following year the club failed to appear but bounced back in 1962.

In 1977 the club moved to the Three Crowns in Bridgwater's St Mary Street and renamed themselves the Crusaders, taking the title from their theme for that year which was *Richard the Lion Heart: The Crusades*. The presentation was popular with the judges and took third place at Bridgwater.

Three years on, and the club had moved from medi-aeval wars to the Civil War of America with their *Johnny Reb*. The entry took second place in Bridgwater. In 1985 they moved once again, this time to the Duke of Monmouth in the High Street and remained there until 2004 when they moved back to their old stamping ground at the Hope Inn.

This is a club which has had its ups and downs but has always known how to enjoy itself. In the early years, its success was in part due to the unstint-ing support of the landlord of the Hope Inn, Fred Cavill. Amongst past members of note are his son, Dennis Cavill, who went on to become the president and now life member of Bridgwater Carnival. Also the Dodden family whose involvement with the club has lasted for generations.

In 2003, Crusaders *brought* Love *to the carnival.*

Globe Carnival Club, Wells

In 1968 the Unigate Carnival Club was formed in Wells under the guidance of Glad Parsons, Bill Baker and various other Unigate employees. Their first entry was *Valhalla, Hall of Dead Heroes*. It was a small affair, certainly by today's standards, with its 4 Kva generator and all completed with a budget of £36. To the delight of the ten members it picked up third place in the local class at Wells Carnival. As the years passed, so the number of Unigate employees in the club diminished. Against this background it was deemed unreasonable for so many non-employees to be on the Unigate site and the club agreed to move. A home was offered by Cyril and Eve Hunt, licencees of the Globe Inn. Having previously used the Rose and Crown and latterly the Mermaid, in 1975 the club became the Globe. Subsequently they have moved to the Wells Rugby Club. The new club's first entry, designed by the late Kevin Sheppard, was *The Spirit of Uncle Sam*. It

was an entry which was to win the Chairman's Choice at Wells Carnival. The club was on its way up, now spending £250 and with a 12 Kva generator. Compare that with today's generators of some 500 Kva.

1979 proved to be a most difficult year. Everything was running behind schedule and the club failed to make it to Bridgwater Carnival with *Midnight in the Nursery*. However, in 1972 Mike O'Neill, a true stalwart of the club, had joined and it was his father, sadly no longer with us, who came to the rescue. Jack O'Neill brought his painting skills to the rescue and the club arrived in time for North Petherton's parade.

Better fortune touched the club the following year when they produced *Guardians of Shangri-La* and it caught the eye of the organisers of London's Easter Parade. During April 1981 the Globe Carnival Club travelled to the capital, complete with

Shamanic Spirit *of 1999.*

Globe's 2003 entry was Nian.

a police escort, to take part in the famous parade. The members had already started dismantling the cart when the Easter Parade committee extended the invitation to be part of their event. At six o'clock on a Thursday morning, the club set off with their float on a low-loader. It was a trip not without incident as motorists reported a Giant Panda flying over the M4 motorway. One of the eleven fibreglass models had disconnected and landed on the eastbound carriageway. It appears that the wind had got under the polythene sheet, which enshrouded the bear, and this resulted in its untimely take off. Imagine the surprise of motorists as they headed towards the capital. With pandas being an endangered species, this was not good news. But their luck was in and the panda survived intact.

At two o'clock that afternoon they arrived safely in the massive car park at Battersea Park. Prior to the procession, safety checks were carried out along the length of the route to ensure that there were no low wires which would impede the progress of the Somerset float. Unfortunately, after the checks had taken place, a local radio station ran a wire across the route and it was lower than the top of the float. A different panda this time had a close encounter, not to mention one of the young ladies on the float. The low wire caught the unsuspecting panda and knocked it of its perch. Thereafter it lay with the young lady trapped beneath it. The situation was recovered and the young lady survived the ordeal uninjured.

It was the only float selected from the Mendip area and so it was with some pride that the members took part. Two coach loads of them and their supporters had gone up for the big day. On the following Tuesday, the float returned home and work began immediately dismantling it ready to start the new year's entry. Three years later they were back in the capital with their *Cosmic Warriors* entry, but this time they had the King William and Mendip Vale Clubs for company.

1984 was something of a landmark year with *Stand and Deliver* achieving top place results around most of the county. Indeed the club were runners up for the County Cup. The idea was based on the life of highwaymen and included an outstanding reproduction stage coach. Come 1990 and the club once again caught the eye of the London scouts and were again invited to attend the Easter Parade with *Dance with the Devil*.

Perhaps their best entry was *Shamanic Spirit* of 1999, based on a Red Indian theme. This two tier

cart was an awesome sight enhanced by the energy of the individual performers. Designed by Tim Durban and Eira Powell, the club was now spending considerably more than in those early years. £22,000 covered the costs including the use of a 360 Kva generator. By the end of that season, the club had collected no fewer than ten trophies for its cabinet, the best trawl up to that time.

In 2001, it just got better. *Automaton* was to take two firsts and two seconds. At their home carnival of Wells it was almost a clean sweep of the trophies and a proud day for club captain Mark Andrews: best artwork; best dance routine; best costume; best local feature. And their year didn't end there. With a royal visit to Wells, celebrating the Queen's Jubilee, the club were chosen to represent carnival.

One name which hasn't been mentioned above and certainly deserves to be mentioned is that of Frank Delaney. Frank is both chairman and a life member of the club and has provided Trojan service in many different areas including the organisation of the team of stewards from the club who provide their services for many local events as an essential fund raiser for the club. Frank is an excellent example of that rare breed who not only dedicates himself to his club, but is willing to share his experience and knowledge with others, irrespective of their allegiance to competing clubs.

In 2003, Globe Carnival Club produced *Nian*, a Chinese theme. Nian is a monstrous dragon-like character from Chinese legend, seriously ugly and ferocious. Its favourite food was humans and it terrorised the occupants of Chinese villages. A wise old man realised that it probably depended on the fear of the people and so he organised the villagers ready for Nian's next visit. On his arrival, they sprang forth, beating drums, burning bamboos and firing crackers. The monster ran until he dropped exhausted. Seizing their opportunity, the villagers slew the dragon and today the Chinese New Year celebrates the defeat of the dragon.

The Globe Club travelled halfway round the world for their next year's theme. In 2004 they produced *Tenochca*. From ancient Chinese culture to ancient Mexico, where 600 years ago, three Aztec kingdoms were united to form the Tenochca Empire in the Basin of Mexico. Each of these entries proved successful with pretty well parallel results; third in Bridgwater, second at Glastonbury and first on their two local circuits of Shepton Mallet and Wells.

Gorgons Carnival Club, Wells

The Gorgons Carnival Club made their first mounted entry in 1973 but prior to that had been a walking club. Previously several of the members had belonged to a tableau club based at the Mendip Hospital in Wells where many of the members worked. Very much a family club in those days, it remains so today with the children of those early members now playing an active part.

Some years ago the club decided to appear as a feature but then a minor revolution took place. It appears that whilst certain members were on holiday, the others decided to change back to tableau. The result was a split between the two camps, tableau and feature. Carnivals came and went with the club failing to appear. As the night of Weston Carnival approached, it was decided to pull out all the stops and Sue Ford, Mike Ford and Maureen Banford dressed as three mythical creatures from the tales of old Greece, the Gorgons. Before long Mike Reed

had joined the throng as Perseus, who had slain the Gorgons and saved the lives of the local villagers. As it happened, the costumes were ready in time for Wells Carnival and, daubed with green poster paints, *Perseus and the Gorgons* made their debut. And that's how it began. The following year, more family and friends came together and formed a committee. The loan of a trailer was agreed and a tractor likewise. Thirty years on, many of those early members still remain with the club.

Whilst appearing mostly as features, in 1992 and 1993 they entered in the comic feature class with *Down on the Farm* and *Cruft's Rejects*. Since then they have been firmly in the feature camp and still await a major result. Recent entries such as *The Night Before*, *Rock DJ* and *Splash* have only been able to achieve lower order results. Nonetheless this is a popular club who understand the spirit of carnival and have produced many excellent floats.

Gorgon's 2003 entry was Splash.

Gremlins Carnival Club, Bridgwater

In 2003 Gremlins presented ?

The Gremlins were formed in 1948 when a group of ex RAF men got together to form a club. Amongst them were John (Dinger) Bell, Ted Lockyer and Chris Allen. Ted came from a carnival background and was the son of the famous Nosey Lockyer who appeared with the Lime Kiln Carnival Club. He was the man who walked the route each year during the war years, carrying a torch, in order to maintain an unbroken tradition. Chris Allen went on to become one time president of Bridgwater Carnival. Dinger Bell's son, Malcolm, also known as Dinger, is currently a life member of the club and his son Tom is currently an active member, completing three generations. In addition Dinger Junior's wife and mother have both been dressmakers. This reflects well the family atmosphere that exists with the Gremlins Carnival Club.

In the RAF, when anything went wrong, the problem was blamed on the Gremlins and therein lay the title for the new club, the RAFA Gremlins. It was a mixed male and female club, somewhat unusual in those days. In later years, the RAFA prefix was dropped as the balance of members became mostly non ex-RAF. Their first song scena was *Pages of Rhythm* and proved an instant success by taking the stage cup. At the end of the year, the club had its first dinner at which it was announced that

under each members plate was the change from their subscriptions. The cost of the costumes had been deducted and the difference refunded. Such practice would be unheard of these days.

It then took the club until 1956 to repeat that initial stage success with *Nursery Fantasy*, but still no success on the road. In 1958 a lack of membership and funds resulted in the club not appearing but they bounced back in 1959. The next twelve years brought mixed fortunes reaching as high as second and as low as twelfth on the road, with similar results on the stage. During those years, the club moved from their Bunch of Grapes headquarters to the Crown Inn. Then in 1971 came the clubs first procession championship with *Carnival, Tijuana Style*. With second on the stage it was an outstanding year – but there was yet the best to come.

1972 was a bitter sweet year. The club knew they had built a great float and were hopeful of a major success. At Bridgwater they took a disappointing second place, beaten by the Ramblers with *Showband*. But the Gremlins results improved as they progressed around the county circuit and after seven carnivals they had enough points to win the best feature cup.

In 1974 they turned their thoughts to Christmas and produced *Land of the Santas*. It was

Galactic Guardians.

an idea which was to win the stage cup but could do no better than fifth on the road. Despite that poor start at Bridgwater, the club went on to take four first places on the rest of the circuit and to win the county cup. Then the following year came the double. Having moved to the Railway Club, popularly known as The Shack, *The World of Hans Christian Anderson* took first place on both road and stage. It was a very enjoyable period at the Shack and one of the popular traditions, during those years, when it was all male membership, was to have the wives perform on the last night of the concerts. Back at the Shack, the good ladies would take to the stage and perform the club's stage show!

In 1978 the Gremlins produced one of those stunning entries about which carnivalites will still be talking for at least a generation later. It was the all blue and silver *Galactic Guardians*, featuring a space ship. It was the first float to be designed without a conventional low level chassis. Take a look at the picture above.

The space craft was supported on high wheeled legs at front and rear in such a way that it was possible to drive a car through the float from one side to the other beneath the main float structure. This was a really adventurous design and one which nearly didn't come off. The design resulted in a lack of stability which presented itself at the eleventh hour

during the early attempts to move the float. However, the problems were overcome by introducing a double axle at the front and the club went on to win the county cup. In many ways, it is surprising that no one else has attempted anything as innovatively different as this brave design. Over the years, we have seen tractors replace horses, generators replace paraffin torches and roofs being added to the float design. But there has been nothing in float design that has taken such a revolutionary approach as that Gremlin design of a quarter of a century ago.

In 1981 the club moved headquarters once again, this time to the Newmarket Hotel where they stayed for the next nine years. In 1983 first place was taken once again with the *Circus Comes To Town*. It was another County Cup Winning entry with a string of successes. But it was so nearly a disaster. The float had pulled into Parkway for the start of the procession. With two trailers and a big steam organ, the tractor pulled away to take the float into the competition. The tractor pulled forward with a grinding sound and the two trailers stayed behind, unmoved. A pin had come loose and the tractor had pulled the turntable out from under the first float. The front of the float had dropped and dug itself into the Tarmac of the road. Conveniently, a local resident arrived with a digger. This was brought forward and used to lift the front of the float. Empty cans and blocks of timber were used to prop the float up whilst the turntable was reversed back into position and the float re-assembled. Whilst this was going on, the other entries were being guided past the Gremlins marooned entry until, as the last one passed, the Gremlins float was fixed in the nick of time. Twisted metal was straightened as best as possible and covered with someone's curtains which David and Gay Squires had miraculously produced. Now at the back of the procession, they entered the route and were rewarded with first place. Further successes around the county circuit brought home the County Cup.

At the club dinner that year, Dave 'Ginger' Smith was presented with the 'Cock Up Cup' for his involvement in the failed turntable. The award is now awarded on an annual basis and creates a lot of good humour. Gremlins have an excellent record for winning trophies but this is one the members prefer to avoid!

In 1991, another move took them to the Bridgwater Snooker Centre and the move heralded an amazing string of success between 1991 and 1995, Star Fighters, Min_____ Morning of the Dragon, Redskins and Pi_____ an unbroken run of Bridgwater first_____ and similarly either overall county ch_____ or best feature.

Indeed in a ten year period, they took first place at Bridgwater no fewer than nine times. An absolutely amazing record and one that will be very hard to beat, if it ever is.

Recent years have seen a continuation of the amazingly high standards which the Gremlins set, albeit the competition from other clubs, Masqueraders in particular, has intensified. 1998's *This is Halloween* took first at Bridgwater, Wells, Glastonbury, joint first at Burnham, with second

Morning of the Dragon *from Gremlins Carnival Club.*

Starfighters.

places at North Petherton and Weston-super-Mare. Not quite enough to win the County Cup. 1999 brought the County Cup back to the Gremlins trophy cabinet as *Afrika* swept the board. In 2000 their entry of *Circus 2000* shared the County Cup with Masqueraders. In 2001 and 2002, *Sinbad* and *Firework Celebration* took the runners up cup for the county circuit having achieved a series of firsts and seconds in each case, beaten again by their old rivals Masqueraders.

Their 2003 entry *Joseph* which was one of the most colourful and vibrant floats in the procession, took third place in Bridgwater, beaten by both Marketeers and Ramblers. Over the county circuit they slipped to fourth place. This is no reflection on the standard of the Gremlins entry. It's just that every now and then, other clubs take a leap forward. Gremlins remain one of the strongest clubs on the circuit and quite capable of re-capturing the County Cup.

Indeed, in 2004 they bounced right back with a vengeance. *Rio Carnival Nights* took a well deserved first place on the stage with the dazzling costumes and energetic performance. With a slight change of title, *Rio* took first place on the road at Bridgwater giving them the overall championship cup. But Masqueraders were their bogey club once again, pipping them to the post at the remaining carnivals except Weston-super-Mare where Gremlins reversed the positions at the top and in so doing deprived Masqueraders of the overall county championship which went instead to the tableau from Gemini Carnival Club.

To produce the fabulous floats we associate with the Gremlins requires the highest standard of engineering and an awful lot of money. The Gremlins have several well-tried methods for raising funds. They have one of the most popular quizzes in the area. Teams even travel from surrounding counties to join in. Their secret of success is to run just one per year but do it really well. Stewarding at Glastonbury Festival is another source but perhaps they are best known for their outside catering services at event such as 'Yesterday's Farming' where they will be found serving meals and drinks inside a huge marquee. It's hard work but they all enjoy it, especially the oc   al race up the tent poles, a favourite activit   farmers.

Sinbad *2001*.

Griffens Carnival Club, Bridgwater

In 2001, the Griffens went SCUBA diving.

The Griffens Carnival Club, whose current head-quarters are at the Squibb Inn in Bridgwater, was formed in 1968 by nine employees at the local Clark's shoe factory. It was as a comic feature that they made their first entry with *The Great Pink Elephant Hunt*. Terry Clare and Mike Holderness were the front and back of the elephant which was chased through the streets of Bridgwater by big game hunter Dave Riddle and a band of 'natives'. If Dave Riddle's version of the story is true, almost immediately after the procession their hired costumes were on a train to a shop in London as they had to be back by 11 o'clock that night!

1971 was a significant year for two reasons. One was that it was the first year of the Bath Bridge Carnival Club which, after five years of taking part in the carnival, were to merge with the Griffens in 1976 when they produced their *War, Love and Peace* entry. The other was that it was the year in which Griffens made their stage debut with *A Load of Old Tom Cobley's*. Their road entry that year was entitled *Barney Bullfrog and His Band* and was the first float to be mechanically propelled. They were a welcome fresh face to the Bridgwater Town Hall stage. They have provided some wonderful stage shows over the years and are notable for their injections of humour and cameo images. It didn't take long for success to

come. In 1980 they took top honours with their stage show *It's Magic*.

The 1970s had already seen much success for the club. In 1972 and the next two years they completed a hat trick of County Cup championship wins in the comic feature classes with *Runaway Train*, *Gnomeward Bound* and *Cinderfellas*. This final theme depicted a fire engine which used a smoke machine fuelled by oily rags. Ironically it caught fire – and so did one of the members! In 1975 the club entered the open feature class with *Ghost Riders* and this move from comic to open feature positioned them to join the elite band of the Bridgwater Gangs and Features who also take part in the carnival concerts. They were by now building their floats at the Henry Fielding at Dunball, now the Admiral's Table. It was to be the last year that Griffens and the Bath Bridge were to enter as separate entities.

In the 1976 procession the clubs had merged to produce *War, Love and Peace* which was to take first place in the open features, success which was repeated the following year despite near disaster when gale force winds stripped the tarpaulin covers from the scaffolding under which the cart was being constructed. Several of their models were destroyed. Nonetheless, the float was finished on

77

2002 Mediaeval Pageant *from the Griffens Carnival Club.*

time and the Bath Bridge Griffens took first place in the open features. Success came again the following year with *Warlords of Destiny*. That particular entry saw the successful pioneering of a new material to the world of carnival, fibreglass. This was to revolutionise model-making and dramatically reduced the destructive effects of inclement weather on the carnival models, most of which were previously constructed using papier mache.

In 1979 they joined the local gangs and features and appeared in the local class for the first time, also now taking their regular spot in the carnival concerts. Griffens have a huge reputation for colour and humour in their stage performances. By the time they produced their second stage show in 1980 with *It's Magic*, they had reached the number one spot. They have been unable to reach such dizzy heights again but have been knocking on the door of success on a regular basis.

In 1989 disaster nearly struck once more. Just days before the big procession, thieves broke into their store at the Henry Fielding Inn and stole a thousand lamp holders, hundreds of feet of electric cable, jigsaw cutters, drills, angle grinders and even an arc welder. An appeal immediately went out to the other clubs for the use of their equipment. In

true carnival spirit, the other clubs responded and the show went on the road, despite their spare welder blowing up just when they thought the situation was coming back under control. Working twenty-four hours a day under spotlights brought them back onto schedule.

The club has continued to be one of the most successful on the circuit, always knocking on the door of major success. Their entries are consistently among the most artistic on the circuit displaying a wealth of talent. In 2001 their *Surf's Up* came fourth overall across the county championship. The 2002 *Mediaeval Pageant* was full of life and colour and typically picked up results between third and fifth whilst the 2003 *Divali* also floated around fourth place. This club is a future winner in waiting.

2004 was perhaps the Griffen's most successful season with their awesome entry of *Hellraisers*. Competing against County-Cup-regular winners like the Masqueraders and Gremlins Carnival Clubs, Griffens took third place at North Petherton, the first time that all the big clubs come together, head to head. It is only a question of time. Someone before long will knock Gremlins and Masqueraders off the top spots – Griffens could be the club to do it.

Above Divali *on the road and below* Bollywood *on the stage.*

2004 Hellraisers *from the Griffens Carnival Club.*

Lime Kiln Carnival Club, Bridgwater

Lime Kiln Carnival Club is one of Bridgwater's oldest surviving clubs and one of only two in the town still using its original headquarters. A 1934 entry was the *Highwaymen* but then a gap appears until 1937 and 1938 when two further entries are recorded. However, the present club dates back to the year after the Second World War when the late Fred Snow, former club president and a life member, was a founder member along with one of carnival's best known characters Bill Biffen. Fred had also served as president of the Somerset Gangs and Features Association. The Lime Kiln Club's glory years were very much in the 1950s and 1960s with a string of top places.

1948 saw first place honours with the *Henry Morgan and His Buccaneers*. The success was repeated in the following two years with *Stepsons of France* and *King Carnival*, the latter also taking first place on the stage. In the twenty years from 1948 to 1967, Lime Kiln took first place honours no fewer than twelve times and also took the stage cup on four occasions in the same period. In the 1950s

and 1960s, they won the overall County Cup three times and in addition won the Midsomer Norton Cup seven times as the best feature across the county circuit. That's an amazing run of victories. Those successes included one of carnival's earliest unashamed sequels with *The Sons of Henry Morgan* in 1967. As if by way of punishment for producing such a blatant repeat, a dry spell of nine years followed until in 1976 *The Music Men* took the top spot on the road and in 1979 *The Chinese Water Garden* took top honours on the stage. Since then the club has been consistently out of the frame but remain much respected and have produced some wonderful performances.

An event worthy of note and now often forgotten is the part which the Lime Kiln Carnival Club took in maintaining the tradition of Glastonbury Carnival. In 1963 the Glastonbury Carnival nearly folded. In order to maintain the tradition, just two floats took part, one was the carnival queen and the other, Lime Kiln Carnival Club.

This club over the years has produced some of

Lime Kiln present The Pride and The Glory.

2003's entry Upendi.

John Owens, present treasurer and secretary of the County Association.

the best known personalities in carnival. Bill Biffen, a founder and life member, has served as president of Bridgwater Carnival and is well known throughout the area. John Owens, yet another life member also now serves as the treasurer and secretary for the Somerset County Guy Fawkes Carnivals Association, a most demanding role.

The pictures on the previous page and above depict their 1992 entry *The Pride and the Glory* and their 2003 entry *Upendi* which took sixth place at Bridgwater. The 1992 entry was based on those very English icons of John Bull, Chelsea Pensioners, Tower of London Beefeaters and the Union Flag. Notice how the red, white and blue have been picked out in the ceiling lights on the canopy of wheels.

Marketeers Carnival Club, Bridgwater

Sydenham origins

In 1959, two juvenile entries took to the road for the first time at Bridgwater Carnival. Rod Stoodley, who in later years was to become one of Bridgwater's most influential carnival secretaries, was the leader of one which presented *Dartmoor's Annual Outing*. Meanwhile, Mel Dando and Company entertained with *Emergency Ward 10*. That company included a certain Gerrard (Chunky) Dunster. Between them, they took the first two places in the juvenile entries. Members from each of the groups recognised the potential benefits of combining their resources, not least of which was that one day they could perhaps compete with Bridgwater's best major feature clubs. From this fusion of energies was born the Sydenham Carnival Club, based at the 'Nissen hut' Sydenham Community Centre, created from the conversion of two war-time pre-fabricated bungalows.

Charlie Swain, Charlie Mockeridge and Ron Rawles were members of the committee. Charlie Mockeridge suggested the idea of forming a carnival club and Rod Stoodley was informed of the idea. He spoke to his good friend Chunky and shortly after the Sydenham Carnival Club was formed with its committee duly appointed. Its first ever president was the Reverend Father Gill, priest at the nearby Saxon Green church, reflecting the community aspect of this venture. Rarely, if ever, before or since, has a parish priest acted as the figurehead for a carnival club. The young Rod Stoodley was appointed captain.

Gay Hawaiians

An enthusiastic programme of fund raising provided sufficient to produce their first entry of *Gay Hawaiians*. The use of a tractor was offered and accepted. Bryan Villis offered his services as electrician and the show was coming together. One club's misfortune was another's blessing. In 1958 the Hardy Spicer Club had disbanded and bequeathed their carnival cart to the first new club to form in their wake. Sydenham were the grateful recipients.

That October, the young club members,

A Marketeer classic – The Land of Make Believe.

Marketeers declared 'Oh, no it isn't'.

supported by grass-skirted young ladies, took to the Town Hall stage during the carnival concerts. They were awarded fourth position, a remarkable result for a new and young club. Their success on stage was followed by fifth place on the road. That credible first year was followed by the *Hystymen* and *Negro Slaves* in 1961 and 1962. Whilst their results on the road were in decline, their 1962 entry took them to third place on the stage. But the club was growing and maturing. The membership wanted pub-based headquarters closer to the town centre. The community centre felt unable to support the club any longer and in 1963 they failed to appear.

They bounced back in 1964 as the Duke of Monmouth Carnival Club and later as the Commercial Inn from 1966 to 1972. By this time they were knocking on the door of success. In their last five years as the Commercial Inn, they achieved third place three times in the Bridgwater processions. Then came the breakthrough.

Success

1972 brought the club's first major trophy with *Bulldog Breed* taking the prestigious first place, success which was repeated the following year with *The Arrival of the Sun Lords*. For the last thirty years,

Marketeers has been one of Bridgwater's most successful clubs, rarely out of the top four positions on stage or road. In 1978 they produced *X-Cert* which took the top spot on the stage, the first time in their history. This was closely followed by a disappointing fifth place on the road at Bridgwater, with the same theme but a different title – *Horrient Express*. The stage success was well deserved. The members had gone to considerable lengths to give their performance every ounce of authenticity, including twelve of the members visiting a dental surgeon in order to produce dental moulds used to create the vampires' fangs.

The Rat Pack

Marketeers have always been a sociable club who know how to enjoy themselves both on and off the stage. On their evenings out, their members are very distinctive in the red jacket uniform. It began in 1979 with a young Steve Wood and Martin Hodge. It was the era of punk bands and the Boomtown Rats led by Bob Geldof. Steve in particular was a fan. Within the club, a young clique had developed to which the older members referred as the Boomtowns. Behind locked doors, the youngsters accepted the label and pursued their own agenda. Martin's mother produced a fluffy red jacket for each of the young group, and Steve Woods added the Boomtown Rats motif. On the first night of the carnival concerts, the club gathered at their Valiant Soldier headquarters. (It was once called the Market House Inn, hence the name of the club.) A calm descended on the room as, one by one, a score or so of the younger members disappeared, later to return wearing their now familiar red jackets. The tradition has survived the years and new members proudly put on their Rat Pack jackets.

The 1980's entry *The Old Brigade on Parade* and the especially memorable 1982s *Land of Make Believe*, both took first place on the road and the latter provided the double by also taking first place on stage, a success which was to be repeated three years later with *Just Clowning Around*. But it was that 1982 entry which has to be viewed as the club's finest success. The music itself, *Land of Make Believe*, was one of those memorable numbers that is remembered years later. The club swept up every trophy for which they qualified, right around the entire county circuit. It was carnival's equivalent of the Grand Slam and World Cup rolled into one.

Riding on the crest of a wave, life has a way of bringing you down to earth, often with a bump. The following year's *Butterfly Ball* deservedly took first place on the stage and the cart was promising. Then disaster struck when a fire on the cart resulted in a loss of lighting and the resultant eighth place. Their 1998 entry of *Moscow State Circus* took third place at Bridgwater, North Petherton and Burnham and was an excellent portrayal. In 2000 and 2001, *Oh No It Isn't* and *Next Stop Clown Town* were both successful enough to take third place for the County Cup in the features' class.

The clown theme is a well worn one in carnival and it takes imagination and a strong understanding of theatre to bring a sense of originality to such a theme. Marketeers achieved that. Instead of simply clowning around, they depicted the creation of a new town well. Clowns from a variety of trades contributed to the work force with a doctor, mayor and a painter amongst the team who made their way by car, train or plane to the town where nothing made sense.

Rock 2003 *from the Marketeers.*

The 2003 entry was *Rock 2003*. This was carnival at its best, a float brought to life by the energy and enthusiasm of the performers. This could so easily have been a County Cup winner but could only take second place at Bridgwater beaten by Rambler's *Midnight Express,* and in fairness another stunning entry. In the open class at Bridgwater, the Masqueraders club had taken first spot with their entry of *Rise of the Machines*. At North Petherton, the two clubs came head to head. North Petherton has always been viewed as difficult for Bridgwater clubs. Marketeers came a disappointing third. However, two nights later at Burnham-on-Sea, they took the top spot against all comers. Second at Shepton Mallet was followed by firsts at Wells and Glastonbury, and a second to finish the season at Weston. They were runners up to Masqueraders as the best feature in the county. From a personal viewpoint, I felt they deserved better.

I especially liked their 2004 stage show *Platoon*, depicting a contingent from the US Army and was disappointed with its fourth place. Performing one particular song, they used projected battleground images from conflicts in which the US Army has seen action. It was brave, brilliant and extremely poignant, one of the best expressions of theatre I have seen on the Town Hall stage. It was dark and sombre and brilliantly portrayed. But in an eight minute show you have to lift the audience back up and that was skilfully done through the use of songs which gently lifted the spectator from the solemnity of war in Vietnam to the cheerful marching GI. The reaction from some who viewed it was one of distaste. It wasn't carnival, they argued. But it was brilliant theatre and as a technique others will be quick to follow.

Out and about
The Marketeers occasionally go on tour or on a trip to a special event. I remember once, on my way to Gatwick airport, my wife and I stopped at the Fleet motorway services. As I stood in the services, a group of hippies entered, dressed in Carnaby Street 1960's style flowing trousers and Kaftan jackets, complete with flowers in their hair. It was like entering a time warp. One came and stood beside me and then a quiet voice said 'Alright, Rog? Where are you off to then?'. It was none other than Chunky Dunster. If I remember correctly the club were on their way to a cricket match, a regular trip for the club. On such trips, it is not unusual for strange things to happen!

At Lords in 1983, two members entered the Long Room, allegedly with the intent of stealing the Ashes. Ten minutes later they emerged, not with the sacred Ashes but with several trays of cakes and sandwiches. At Hove in 1989, one club member fell asleep in the stands under a pile of newspapers. An attempt to cremate him by setting fire to the papers

was unsuccessful but later that same day, allegedly, twenty Marketeers were seen running around the promenade at Brighton – naked! At Trent Bridge in 1989, after Vic Marks hit the winning run for Somerset, Garry Chedgey, according to his own words when he described the event at the club's fortieth anniversary, followed Vic into the Somerset dressing room and a few minutes later reappeared on the balcony flanked by those cricketing legends Viv Richards and Joel Garner. At Bath in 1990, the club were interviewed on Sky TV, dressed as Romans.

Later that day, heavy rain stopped play and the rainwater butt which collected the rain from the large beer tent, was overflowing. Someone, who was doing a very good impersonation of Ghandi, was found swimming in the butt.

Perhaps their cheekiest venture in all these episodes was at Glamorgan in 1992. The club arrived dressed as Morris Dancers. One of the club managed to convince the ground staff that they were the half time entertainment and the whole club got in for free. The stories go on but free entertainment is what the Marketeers are all about and at the heart of it all is the living legend, that founder member, Chunky Dunster.

Living legend
Chunky Dunster, whose real name is Gerrard, is a painter by trade. Today he remains actively involved with the club as its president and throughout his carnival career has been an example to us all as to how to play the game in the true spirit of

The legendary Chunky Dunster.

(Photo courtesy www.Bridgwater-photos.co.uk)

Marketeers 2004 entry was Platoon.

carnival. He has always been, and remains, a great ambassador to carnival – with perhaps one exception. I return to cricket at Lords and the Gillette Cup semi final. Marketeer Dave Stone played the last post on his bugle as each opposition wicket fell. But more noticeable even than that distinctive bugle call was the one-man invasion of the pitch. Those watching at home on TV heard Richie Benaud remark 'We have an idiot on the pitch.' In Chunky's home, young Gregg Dunster commented 'Quick, Mum. Dad's on the telly!' Suzette watched as the camera followed the invader, her eyes on the crowd behind the intruder, hoping to spot her husband amongst the crowd. The invader tripped and tumbled. As his hat fell off to reveal his distinctive fleshy head, Suzette instantly recognised the 'idiot' as one very familiar to her. It was with some pride that Chunky boasted that he had received a rollicking from no less a celebrity than Sir Garfield Sobers.

But it has to be said that Chunky has dedicated himself to carnival and deserves to be recognised for his commitment and enthusiasm. So perhaps it came as no surprise to discover that Chunky was noticed when a government initiative was set up to develop a strategy to improve the quality and range of cultural activity available to those living in the South West. It was headed up by *Culture South West* who commenced the consultative process. As an early initiative they looked to identify where regional culture already successfully existed and thrived. Clearly in Somerset, the carnivals are the largest expression of local culture. Digging deeper, they searched for examples of those individuals who are the keystones to the survival of such culture. What makes them tick? How can we replicate this elsewhere?

What they found was Chunky, one of carnival's great characters. Other leading lights in other parts of the South West were likewise discovered. Think of all those other expressions of regional culture; Padstow's Hobby Horse, Bournemouth's Symphony Orchestra, Bristol's Old Vic Theatre, Sidmouth's Folk Festival, Glastonbury's annual music festival and of course the Somerset carnivals. All these and more were reviewed by *Culture South West*. The result of the whole exercise was the production in 2001 of a government backed cultural strategy for the South West entitled *In Search of Chunky Dunsters*. The legend lives on.

Masqueraders Carnival Club, Glastonbury

Unarguably one of the most successful clubs on the carnival circuit, the Meare-based Masqueraders Carnival Club was founded in December 1985 when a group of friends, mostly Young Farmers, floated the idea of forming a club. An approach to the land-lord of the Countryman Inn met with a favourable response and the newly formed band set about increasing their numbers with family and friends. The decision was soon made to appear as a comic feature and to attend the Somerset County Circuit, the big seven, plus Midsomer Norton.

Carol singing, discos, raffles, barbecues, clay pigeon shoots, race nights, selling fresh milk at Glastonbury Festival and even a rodeo have all been part of the Masqueraders fund raising activities. An awful lot of energy went into raising the funds for that first year's entry entitled *Pass the Port – Blub, Blub, Blub*. The effort had all been worthwhile with this newly formed club taking various positions from first to fourth around the 1986 circuit but sufficiently consistent to take the County Cup honours in the comic feature class.

It served as an alarm bell to the other clubs that this newcomer with just twenty five members could produce such a credible first year's entry. And to add to the success, they were even invited to attend the following year's Easter Parade in London. Following their initial success, the club saw little point in playing again in the second division. They decided to compete with the big boys in the non comic features, a decision that with hindsight no one can regret. 1987 to 1989 saw mixed fortunes with results ranging from first to tenth at the various carnivals.

Since 1989 they have rarely been out of the frame. With increasingly challenging floats, top of the poll results became more consistent despite a few difficult moments. Their 1990 entry came runner up to Gremlins for the County Cup. The 1992 entry of *Chen* hit problems as soon as it arrived in Bridgwater. On turning a tight corner during the line up process, a dragon's head buckled as one section of the entry jack-knifed into the other. Once the procession was over, the float was left overnight in the collection zone for North Petherton carnival and this time was vandalised with several thousands of pounds worth of sound equipment stolen. Undeterred they persevered and with a string of firsts and seconds were runners up for the County Cup.

The next three years saw similar success but slowly slipping down through the county cup rank-ings with second, third and then fourth. Perhaps the Bridgwater clubs had got off their laurels. Maybe it was due to the disruption which resulted from being served with an eviction order which

declared that all float building should stop at the Countryman Inn, albeit the club still remains with the inn as their headquarters. A generous offer to use land for a year at Middleton Engineering was gratefully accepted. Then the Abbey Moor Peat Works came to the rescue and finally came the welcome news that planning permission had been granted for a permanent building ground with shed space, allowing the clubs to build all year round.

From that point on, the club saw a return to winning form with the memorable 1996 *Intergalactic Circus*. First places were awarded everywhere except for Wells where it was a second, but it was sufficient to win the Midsomer Norton Cup in the features class. Then came 1997 when the club swept the board with EFX, a clean sweep marred only by sharing first place at Shepton Mallet, a result which deprived them of the half a point required to be the overall county champions. In 1998, the dream finally came true when they were crowned overall champions of the county with *Live at Las Vegas*,

Vandals stripped out Masqueraders sound system.

2000 saw Masqueraders celebrate with Mill-Looney-Um.

sweeping the board with seven first places, only sharing the honour once with Gremlins at Burnham.

1999 saw them in second place for the County Cup, beaten by their old rivals Gremlins. The following year they shared, with Gremlins, the county cup honour with their cartoon based entry *Mil-looney-um 2000*. In 2001 their stunning entry of *Jack's Back*, brilliantly lit with over 20,000 light bulbs, and strikingly effective with just two basic colours, ensured they were once again outright winners.

Honours for the County Cup were shared with the tableau from Huckyduck when Masqueraders produced *Whizzball* in 2002 but was won outright again with *Rise of the Machines* in 2003. That particular race was a close run thing. Shambles Carnival Club had started their season with a third place at Bridgwater, dropping two points, but then had an unblemished run of firsts in the tableau class. Meanwhile, Masqueraders dropped a point at Burnham and again at Wells, where second places

broke their run of firsts. As the two clubs entered Weston for the final and deciding carnival, the County Cup hung in the balance. When the results were announced, Shambles had been awarded first place, but jointly with Wills Carnival Club. That cost them half a point and a share of the County Cup. Masqueraders maintained their winning run.

Few people in carnival understand the vagaries of the judging system at Weston-Super-Mare. But overwhelmingly the carnival fraternity view it with suspicion. Whilst 2003 worked in their favour, the 2004 result worked against the Masqueraders. At each of the first six carnivals, Masqueraders had taken first with their entry and Gemini had taken first in the tableau class. Entering Weston, the two clubs were in line to share the County Cup honours. But there were few who believed that would happen. And so it turned out to be that Gremlins took first place, with Masqueraders second, leaving Gemini as the clear winner for the overall championship.

Masqueraders remain one of the county's largest clubs with typically sixty members plus forty or so supporters. Dave Churches and Pete Hill are now the only two remaining original members.

You have only to look at a Masquerader float in procession to know that there is a great strength of engineering talent within the club, coming from highly talented figures like the charismatic John Thompson who has now had thirty years or more involvement with carnival. It is thanks to people like those mentioned that the Masqueraders are noted for the enormity and vibrancy of their floats, a true spectacle of movement and colour.

The stunning duo-chromed Jack's Back *of 2001.*

Above: Rise of the Machines. *Below: 2004* Heyoka Shamanic Warriors.
Both from the Masqueraders Carnival Club.

Mendip Vale Carnival Club, Wells

Mendip Vale's 2003 entry was Jester Show.

Life began in 1962 for the Mendip Vale Carnival Club when a number of employees from the local Unigate factory got together. Amongst their founder members were Bill Baker (now a member of Globe Carnival Club) and Willy Harris. The Mendip Vale Carnival Club, who have always adhered to the tableau discipline, can boast a string of results in the top three at their home circuits but in recent years have lacked that same level of success on the open circuit. But they have had their moments and tasted success. In 1979 they took second place for the County Cup with their *Crown Jewels*.

In 1984 they took part in the Easter Parade at Battersea Park with their *Ride of the Valkyries* theme. However, they had to lose one of their horses since its total height from ground level was too great for it to pass under some of the bridges on the route. You'd think they'd have known better from the previous year. With the same float, they became stuck under a footbridge during the November processions. It was lined with young schoolboys keen to see the floats go under. As they approached the bridge, the youngsters called to them to stop. 'You're going to hit the bridge! You're too high!' they cried. Too late the driver heard the grinding sound of the carnival float against the bridge structure. They were stuck fast. The tyres were partially deflated, timber structures removed from the top of the float and steel work sawn away. Still they could not budge. Finally they let the tyres down to the rim and slowly they just scraped under the bridge.

Imagine the grin on those schoolboy faces as the float limped the half mile up the road to a petrol filling station which offered an airline to re-inflate all the tyres. This is a club which clearly has a problem with dimensions. Back in 1965 they appeared in Shepton Mallet with *Those Magnificent Men in their Flying Machine* with aircraft whose wings were definitely shorter than they had been at the previous three carnivals. Their wingspan previously was such that, unbelievably, as they approached Shepton Mallet they got stuck between two lamp posts.

It will come as no surprise to hear that the club motto is 'Win or Lose, plenty of booze.' Keith Sheppard, popularly known as Mini, has been the tractor driver for the club for thirty-one years and now his son has joined the team. At eighteen years old, he drove his first carnivals at North Petherton and Shepton Mallet. According to Mini, their greatest recent success was *Voodoo Magic* in 1988. It was a success because it was the last time they actually finished a cart in line with their expectations. But they are, and always have been, a very sociable club. At the time of writing, they have just purchased a new mini bus to take them the the numerous social and carnival events which they attend. To help pay for that, their main fund raiser is the Glastonbury Festival.

In recent years the club, which is now based at the Shurston Inn in Wells, has produced *Christmas Magic*, *Skool's Out*, *Jester Show* and *Palm Beach*.

The North Pole Carnival Club of 1933 portray the Norfolk and Suffolk Borderers of 1831.

Ramblers Carnival Club, Bridgwater

The Ramblers are one of Bridgwater's most successful clubs and one which is full of both character and characters. They have an unparalleled reputation for zany stunts, some which have gone down in carnival legend. Perhaps the most noteworthy was the kidnapping of Camelot, a fibre glass camel. Camelot had entered carnival as part of a Young Farmer's entry in a previous year. After the carnival he was literally put out to pasture. This almost life size model of a camel was placed in a field alongside the M5 motorway to the amazement of passing motorists. He became a talking point, a landmark, long before the Angel of the North or the Willow Man.

Clearly with such celebrity status, he was an easy target for 'terrorist' activity. He was kidnapped – by an apparently secret terrorist group – who happened to be based at the Bunch of Grapes and I can now reveal to be the Ramblers Carnival Club. Naturally a ransom was demanded. The *Bridgwater Mercury* article published on 5 October 1993 referred to the event.

Camelot, Sedgemoor's famous M5 camel, is alive and well, the Mercury *can report, after we were invited to a secret rendezvous with his 'PLO' kidnappers at the weekend. The dromedary and former carnival star, which was kidnapped from his roadside home at East Bower Farm last week, was brought to the rendezvous by a group of masked desperadoes in military uniform. Camelot was in good health and appears to have received a fresh coat of paint. A representative of the 'para-military' organisation handed over a ransom demand to the* Mercury, *which is now being considered.*

Over the weeks that followed, postcards arrived from around the world, apparently from Camelot, stating where he was, for example at the Pyramids in Egypt with some of his long lost family, and stating that he was being well treated. It doesn't take a genius to discover that one of the Ramblers was a travel agent with clients able to go abroad and post back cards allegedly from Camelot. Not only did this episode make the local papers but also the

In 1992 Ramblers joined in the American Parade.

1993 Droids *from the Ramblers.*

local TV news stations. Even Terry Wogan gave regular updates. This apparent association with terrorist organisations was confirmed shortly after when Ramblers, dressed as Palestinians, were seen praying to Allah as they faced Mecca. They were actually kneeling on the steps of the local Mecca cinema.

If you have ever witnessed a Highland fling on the steps of Admiral Blake's statue, or seen a 6 foot fox being hunted through the town by huntsmen in evening dress, or watched with amazement as a group of cyclists passed through the White Hart Hotel, or seen traffic stopped in St John Street whilst an inter club tug-o-war competition was held, then you have probably witnessed a Rambler stunt.

So who can we blame for the creation of such an extrovert bunch. It all began in 1961 when Mike Hancock, Terry Milton, Roy Turner, Dave Bennett, Pete Edmonds, Plum Pardoe, Brian Sweeting, Dave Baker, Dave Bennett and Jessy Howes gathered together. Over forty years on, many of those members are still actively involved, as are the sons of the same. The club based themselves at the Duke

of Monmouth and then moved to the Beaufort Arms in St John Street. For many years now they have been based at the Bunch of Grapes.

1962 brought their first entry, *The Vikings*, which took a very credible third place on the road and seventh on stage. In 1963 they produced *The Gay Guards of India*. Unfortunately the English language has changed such that Gay Guards has a different connotation today, but it 1963 it was far more innocent. That year they came fourth, the next year fifth with the *Capture of the Loch Ness Monster.* It looked as if the promising start was a flash in the pan. But then in 1966 came *Homage to the Abominable Snowman* and first place in the procession and winner of the County Cup. It was to be the first of many over the years. In 1968 with *Mardi Gras Parade*, they slipped to sixth place on the road but came third on the stage with a memorable medley of songs beginning with the especially appropriate opening lines of 'Mardi Gras, the town's alight because tonight the world's a crazy masquerade. In every street the dancing feet are joining in the big parade.' It was a thoroughly popular show and their choice of stage songs, by the end of the concert fortnight, were being sung in every carnival pub in the town. Disappointingly it only brought them third place but the promise was there and the following year, 1969, *Sacrificial Fantasy* took the stage honours.

In 1970 it just got better with *Minstrel Magic*, a perennial favourite in those days, taking first on both stage and road. To win the double is exceptional but Ramblers, who in between were to take the County Cup for features in 1970 and 1971, were to repeat that success in 1972 (*Showband*), 1986 (*Caribbean Showtime*) and 1988 (*Circus on Parade*). Their 1986 win on the road, which was completed by taking the overall County Cup for the second time, was the start of a run of four consecutive wins, 1986 to 1989, the first club ever to achieve such a run. That run included County Cup successes in 1987 and 1988. As a record it has in fact been beaten since by their old rivals the Gremlins, but nonetheless remains an outstanding achievement.

In more recent years fortunes have been mixed. 1994's *Rhythm of the Sun* failed to complete the circuit at Bridgwater as the result of a fire, but the first place was their reward for the stage show. In 1996 they repeated the stage success with *Dragons*. 1998's *Piracy* took second at Bridgwater and Glastonbury with three thirds elsewhere.

Since then, they have re-found their winning form. Their 2001 entry of *Lion King* was quite stunning and perhaps would have done better than its second place if technical problems had not struck early in the procession. But 2002 saw them with first place honours at Bridgwater with the truly awesome *Invasion Force*, which also took third place in the race for the County Cup. First place at Bridgwater was repeated with the *Midnight Express*, an entry which also brought them first place on the stage. Across the county they again came third in the county championship. This is a club which won't lie down – unless it's to block the road or some other zany stunt. You have been warned!

Two of Ramblers' Pirates buckle their swashes in 1992.

Ramblers' Midnight Express.

For many years now the Ramblers have built their floats on the site of the Morganians Rugby Club. They have a wide range of fund raising activities. These include cabaret nights and their very popular quiz nights. One of the most popular acts in the cabarets, although sadly seen no more, was the club's own rock band called Rambling On. This was made up from some of the exceptionally talented members of the club, such as club stalwarts Terry Pope, Vince Houlighan, Martin Paisey and Barry Saunders, who reproduced music from the sixties and seventies. It was with great sadness that the local population heard of the end of the group. They did however manage to stage more final and come back performances than Frank Sinatra. Funds are also raised by acting as stewards at the Glastonbury Festival.

The club remains one of the most successful on the circuit with a large and loyal membership. It is also well blessed with a particularly strong vice presidents organisation which assists greatly in both financial and practical contributions.

Renegades Carnival Club, Bridgwater

Life began in 1966 for the Renegades Carnival Club. Roger Evans, David Elson, Jim Bartlett, Albert Ford and a few others, got together and discussed forming a carnival club. With the exception of myself, they all worked at the Wellworthy piston manufacturing plant in Bridgwater. The company agreed that the newly formed club could use its large car-parking area as a site on which the club could build its float.

During the autumn of 1966, the members met at the King William Inn, popularly known as the King Billy. It was too late to enter the 1966 carnival but in plenty of time to start the fund raising for the following year. A weekly raffle held within the factory was organised and once a week Albert Ford sat in a cubicle of the gent's toilets folding raffle tickets ready for the draw. Skittle weekends and jumble sales were the other main fundraisers. After

the third jumble sale, most of the club members were suffering from flea bites and it was decided never to do a jumble sale again.

The club's first entry was *The Rainmakers*. The theme was based on the Bantain tribe of New Guinea, a tribe who wore extremely high hats in the belief that they could reach the clouds and induce rain. Brown body stocking were used to give the appearance of natives. Albert Ford, however, as the tribal witch doctor, wore a costume of straw from head to foot. This proved too much of a temptation for one spectator in Bridgwater who tried to set fire to the straw whilst Albert was still inside. The club captain swiftly leapt off the cart, inflicted serious pain on the miscreant and the procession continued, the incident almost unnoticed other than by those in the immediate vicinity.

1993 Renegades are in The Movies.

2003 sees the Renegades go all American with 4th of July.

As a theme, it proved relatively successful. On the stage, this new club took fourth place, an unexpected success against the more established clubs. The success was entirely down to the use of a choreographer – Madge Hewitt of the Pantomime Society. Other clubs were soon to realise the benefits of choreography and Wellworthy were only once again to reach that fourth spot. During that year there were two incidents which could have led to disaster but were simply hilarious at the time and they both came on the same night. Our headquarters was a riverside pub, on the West Quay, now known as the Royal Marine Club. The night in question, the river was in flood and broke over the banks, which were much lower in those days with no flood defence walls. The muddy waters crossed the road and continuing to rise, came up over the kerb and then over the step into the pub. Once over the front step, it was downhill into the bar and downhill into the yard out the back.

Our changing room was across the yard and the river was beginning to flood it. In the centre of the yard was a drain cover which one member removed believing that a complete river of flood water would disappear down it. Of course it didn't,

in fact the drain led straight back into the river. So now the muddy water had found another way in. The cover wasn't replaced when it came to the time to leave our changing room and head for the stage. One member gallantly offered to carry one of the glamorous dancing girls through the muddy waters so that they could leave the pub. As he crossed the flooded yard, so he disappeared into the open manhole, still with the dancing girl in his arms.

Later that same evening as we returned, and the river was just starting to subside, we walked along the recently flooded quayside, now slippery with a layer of mud, wearing ballet style dancing shoes. The shiny soles of one of our male performers hit a slippery patch and he rocketed forward and flat on his back shot into the river. It was a bedraggled warrior that climbed out of the river with drooping ostrich feathers where once a headdress had been.

On the road, success came in a different form. It rained everywhere, torrentially. It was one of the wettest carnivals on record and *The Rainmakers* received friendly pantomime style boos all the way around the county circuit.

The club was one of the first to have female

members and perhaps because of that has lacked the strength and depth of other clubs established just as long as itself. In 1977, the Wellworthy title was dropped and the club became the Renegades, which it remains to this day. Under the new name, they produced *A Night with the Teds*, an energetic rock and roll performance which remains one of their most enjoyable. It was one of the many times that the *Renegades* won the Most Improved on Stage Cup.

In 1985 tragedy struck. An arson attack resulted in the float being destroyed by fire with just days to go to Bridgwater Carnival. In true carnival spirit, the other clubs, both large and small, rallied around with all forms of support. Materials and lighting equipment rolled in. Engineers, carpenters and painters rallied around. As each club approached the finish of their own float, so members were released to the Renegades and the show went on the road to the cheers of the public who knew how close the club had come to disaster. Today the club remains predominantly a young club with a high proportion of female members. Over the years, it has acted as a training ground for newcomers who have then moved on to join the more successful clubs. In that capacity, it remains a significant club and one that has not lost sight of the spirit of carnival.

Renegades 2004. Chinese Celebrations.

Vagabonds Carnival Club, Bridgwater

Formed in 1947, the Vagabonds Carnival Club have a long and successful pedigree, especially where the stage show is concerned, rarely being out of the frame at any time throughout their history. Perhaps that strength on stage is deeply rooted in their early performances. Ken Parsons, later to become the long standing secretary of Bridgwater Carnival, and Walt Creedy, who in similar fashion became the long serving treasurer of Bridgwater Carnival, were the founder members. In those early days, they rented a room at Unity House in Dampiet Street, the local Labour Party headquarters for one shilling a night (5p). Their first entry in 1948 was *The Miners*. Stan Bevan gave a wonderful and moving rendition of 'Bless this House'. Stan was an amazing singer and later went on to perform for the Sadlers Wells Opera Company. Their position on stage that year is unknown but the procession entry took first place. An amazing start to the newly formed club of just twelve members.

The following year's *Gay Bachelors* slipped to fourth on the road but took first on the stage. The club was then based at the now extinct Railway Hotel and moved to the Bristol and Exeter Hotel in 1951. The move brought a change of fortune as the club took first place in the procession with *Widdicombe Festival Fair*. 1952 to 1955 brought four consecutive first places on the stage and a string of first, second and third on the road.

In 1955 one of their members, Ray Heal, took over Ye Olde Oake Inn in Bridgwater's High Street. He was one of the most popular landlords in town and really looked after his club and its visitors. Indeed, at the rear of the inn was a lean-to former stables. This was cleared out and cleaned up to become the club's headquarters for the best part of a quarter of a century. Meanwhile, in 1956, the club celebrated an amazing first place with their entry *Meatless Tyrants*. What made this so amazing was that it was possibly the cheapest cart ever built.

2003 Bugz. *The stage show.*

1999's Viva Brasil.

They were basically dressed as tramps and the float was built for the total sum of 17s 8d (88p). Financially it was a profitable year with the club winning over £32 in prize money.

The club remained at Ye Olde Oake until 1980, when the Angel Place Shopping Centre was built on the site. During that time they took five first places on the road and dominated the stage show with ten wins. In 1967, they repeated their earlier performance of *The Miners*. It gained first on stage and third on the road, but one memorable night comes to mind. During those days, it was the custom for the clubs to travel each night to the headquarters of other clubs and the combined clubs would sing from early evening into the late hours. There were no juke boxes or discos in those days. It was good singing and for me the best part of the social side of carnival. Unfortunately one night at the Blake Arms, at the headquarters of my own club, the Vagabonds visited us in the spirit of carnival but one member let the side down.

An argument took place and bad language was exchanged in an aggressive manner. The senior members of the Vagabonds took control, calmed the situation down, apologised to the landlord and landlady and took the offending member away. The following evening, as the pub opened, the whole Vagabonds club were waiting outside the Blake Arms, complete with miners' dress and miners' helmets. As one they entered the bar and the club captain asked that the landlord and landlady should both be present as they offered an apology for the previous night's misbehaviour in the best way they knew how. The bar lights were turned off and the miners' helmets lit. The bar glowed in a warm and welcoming way as the Vagabonds, soft and low, sang the most moving rendition of 'Bless this house' that I have ever heard. It was a touching moment. A tear came to the landlady's eye as she thanked the club for the thoughtful way they had redeemed themselves. Gentlemen to the end.

In 1977 and 1979, their entries of *Ragtime Rhythm* and *Y Viva Espana* not only won at Bridgwater but also took the Midsomer Norton Cup on the county circuit as the best feature. When Ye Olde Oake was swallowed up in the development of a shopping precinct, the club managed to keep it in the family by moving to the Rose and Crown, run by Ray Heal's brother, Cyril. It was 1990 before they moved again, this time to the Commercial Inn in Redgate Street where they remain today. 1999's *Viva Brasil* shared second place for the County Cup with Masqueraders, Gremlins winning it. Their 2003 entry was *Bugz* which came fifth and in 2004 *In the Deep* took second place on the stage.

But back on the Town Hall stage, another memorable night from the Vagabonds came during the show when one of their members lost his way on stage. He entered from the wings and flip-flopped across the stage wearing snorkel, mask and huge flippers. Unfortunately his mask had misted up and he was unable to see just where he was going. Believing he was walking across the stage, he walked straight over the front edge and fell into the orchestra pit. Fortunately for him, but not for the drummer, his fall was broken when he landed in the drum.

Past members already mentioned are Ken Parsons and Walt Creedy. Another stalwart worthy of mention is Bill Holland. Bill was made a life member of the Vagabonds and eventually joined the Bridgwater Carnival Committee where he put in years of dedicated service as the collection officer. Having served the maximum term as president of that organisation, he became of life member of Bridgwater Carnival.

In 2004 the Vagabonds became Pirates.

SOMERSET CARNIVALS – A CELEBRATION OF FOUR HUNDRED YEARS

Westonzoyland Carnival Club

The Westonzoyland club, now based at the Sedgemoor Inn in Westonzoyland, first hit the road in 1961 with *Westonzoyland Flintstones*. This was followed by *Keystone Cops* in 1962. In 1963 they appeared as the Shoulder of Mutton Carnival Club with *English Country Garden* and earned themselves second place in the feature class at Bridgwater. There then followed *The Old Mill Stream, Nights of Gladness, Mississippi Memories, Cleopatra Enters Rome, Broadway* and *Festival of Magha Puja* which brought the club a string of firsts and seconds through the remainder of the 1960s. After a relatively dry spell through the 1970s, *Glitter Pillar, Whole World in his Hands* and *Festive Fantasy* each brought home first prizes in 1981-83. Since 1987 when *Ole Ole* also took first place, there has been a bit of a dry spell but the club continues to produce some excellent floats in both the features and comic features classes. In 1999, *Siesta Fiesta* took first place for the County Cup in the comic features class. In 2002 that county cup success was repeated, again in the comic features class, with *Wing Nuts*. A year later, back in the non-comic features class, their 2003 entry was *Wild Wild West* which took eighth place at Bridgwater.

2003 and Westonzoyland Carnival Club go to the Wild Wild West.

Wick Carnival Club

The Wick Carnival Club was formed in 1961 by members who previously had appeared with the local Young Farmers. There first entry was *Mega Ton Maisey*, a high yield milking cow! It was a comic feature, a class which the club were later to abandon in favour of the open feature class.

In 2000, *Yuletide* took a first at Wells and a third at Bridgwater, 2001's *Jackpot* took second at Wells but the following year's *Trick or Treat* slipped to fourth. The club bounced back somewhat in 2003 with *Alabama Bound* taking fourth at Bridgwater, ninth at Burnham and a second at Wells. It was a somewhat controversial year. The club had blacked up their faces in Al Jolson and Black and White Minstrel style. Needless to say, there were individuals who felt this blacking up lacked political correctness and suggestions were made that the club would be referred to the Commission for Racial Equality. Fortunately common sense was allowed to prevail and the club continued with their theme unchanged.

Their 2004 entry of Pantomania was full of fun and achieved mixed results ranging from fourth in Bridgwater to tenth in Burnham-on-Sea.

2003 Wick Carnival Club are Alabama Bound.

YMCA Carnival Club, Bridgwater

It is satisfying to think that the presence of the YMCA Carnival Club in our processions completes a circle. George Williams was born at Ashway Farm in Dulverton in 1821. Aged fourteen he travelled to Bridgwater and took up employment as an apprentice to Henry William Holmes who had thirty such apprentices learning the drapery trade. George was encouraged by his employer to attend the Zion Chapel and there he developed a strong religious conviction that stayed with him throughout his life. During those years with Mr Holmes, working in the shop on the Cornhill, he would have watched the carnival procession going by. He later moved to London, became a successful businessman and there founded the world-wide organisation which we know as the YMCA.

It was in 1968 that Mrs May Oliver, with a small band of young YMCA members, formed their new carnival club. Appearing in the non comic feature class, their first entry was *The Tea Plot* which took fourth place. Next came *Il Gondoliere* followed in 1970 and 1971 by *Cossack Wedding* and *The King and I*, both of which took first place. Then the club joined the big time by becoming members of the Bridgwater Gangs and Features, which meant competing on stage and road with the best of the big clubs.

Since then, their results have never been particularly high other than in 1982 when *Graduation Rhythm* tied for third place. On stage they have faired somewhat better and have always been able to produce enjoyable performances. Their 1979 *High Society Afloat* took first place on the stage and brought the club its well deserved reward. The dizzy height has never since been reached with the

2003 YMCA's Travellin' Show.

YMCA 2004 presented To The Beyond.

club floating around the lower orders, but still enjoying the spirit of carnival as they wait for their day to come once again.

In recent years misfortune has struck the club. In a howling gale, a sheet of corrugated iron was torn from their building shed, hitting a passer by with fatal consequences. It was a tragic occurrence for a club which deserved better fortune. Through this difficult period, club stalwarts Arthur Leigh and his wife Lynne have helped to keep the club together. The club is slowly recovering from that difficult period and in 2003 produced their *Travellin' Show* which came eleventh at Bridgwater,

and twenty-seventh at Burnham. What the results don't tell you is that here was a club which was struggling but rather than take a year out to build up their funds, as some clubs have done in the past, and produce a more competitive entry, they appeared with a much reduced float, one which was within their budget. It was the true spirit of carnival, in which it is the taking part which is most important to the members, rather than the need to win. It was a credible and worthy performance from this small but perfectly formed club, based at the River Parrett Inn. George Williams would have been proud of them.

Young at Heart Pilgrims

The Young at Heart Carnival Club was founded by Gary and Mark Stephens, Darren Hill, Shane Sately, Troy Hill, David Stokes and Julian Smith. David Stokes had previously been a helper with the Westonzoyland Carnival Club and now serves as the publicity officer for the Bridgwater Carnival Committee. Young at Heart started life as a comic feature based at the Sedgemoor Inn, Westonzoyland. They joined carnival in 1986 with *Cat Capers*, an entry which failed to make the frame. With one year's experience under their belt, they showed what they were made of. Well before J. K. Rowling introduced the world to Hogwart's School of Magic, in 1987 Young at Heart produced their winning entry *The School of Magic*. There then followed three years of second places in the comic feature class at Bridgwater with various similar results around the county before they hit the number one spot again in 1991 with *You Little Monkeys*.

The club had a succession of headquarters over the years including The Shoulder of Mutton in Westonzoyland and then moving into Bridgwater to the Rebels Retreat, No Jackets Required and the Cross Rifles. In 1992 the club took a change of tack and appeared for a few years as a non-comic feature with varying results. Their 1995 entry of *Vision 3000* was unplaced at Bridgwater due to light failure but was memorable for the unique propulsion chosen. It went on to take first place in the non-winners class at Weston-super-Mare. Since 1996 the club's fortunes have been somewhat mixed. In 2001 they found themselves having to dispel rumours that the club had folded. It was however to be their last year as just the Young At Heart Carnival Club. The following year they were to merge with the Puriton Pilgrims.

The Pilgrims, who were based at the Puriton Inn, had produced a number of comic feature entries which frequently took first place in the local comic class at Burnham-on-Sea, albeit not up against a great deal of opposition. In the open classes they came further down the order but nonetheless produced many entertaining entries such as 1990's *Flintstone's Holiday*, 1995's *Middle of the House* and 1998's *Star Trekkers*.

Their last entry was on foot, coming seventh at Bridgwater with *Copabanana*. The two clubs merged in 2002 and are now based at the Bridgwater Sports and Social Club. Recent entries have included *Salaam Bombay* and *Satanic*.

Young at Heart's Vision 3000.

Pilgrims go on the Flintstone's Holiday.

In 2003 Young at Heart Pilgrims presented Salaam Bombay.

THE TABLEAUX FROM THE COUNTY CIRCUIT

Centurions Carnival Club

Although Bridgwater could once boast numerous tableau clubs, today the Centurions are one of the only two surviving in the town. The Centurions began life as the Town Council Employees in 1938. Having produced just one entry, war broke out and it was to be another seven years before they reappeared. It was worth the wait for their *Burmese Gentlemen* took first place at Bridgwater, success which the club was to repeat eight more times between 1950 and 1983 including twice winning the County Cup in 1967 and 1973. In like fashion, a string of consecutive first places on the stage were also awarded to the club. Those successes included seven stage cup wins in an eight year period.

The club disbanded for a while, with no entries appearing between 1953 and 1966, but when they came back in 1967 with *Marco Polo,* it was straight into first place. But one of their procession entries nearly failed to make it onto the road. The entry had been built inside a council yard with a large gated entrance. When the time came to take the float to the line up zone, the entry was a few inches too high to go under the arch. They were trapped. The solution was to dig out two shallow troughs where the wheels would run and let a few pounds of pressure out of the tyres, re-inflating them once free of the archway. Near disaster also struck in 1974 when *Egyptian Splendour* was crossing the Westonzoyland Aerodrome on its way to Shepton Mallet. Gale force winds struck causing enormous damage to the float. Members rallied around and, working day and night, completed sufficient repair work to get the cart back on the road.

In 2004 the Centurions were Stargazers.

In 2003 the Centurions invited us to Come To The Circus.

The 1982 entry saw a welcome return to fist place after a six-year gap and *Signs of the Zodiac* was invited to attend the Easter Parade in London. In 1984 the club, following the fashion of the time, changed its name to the Centurions and it was under that name that in 1986 they produced the somewhat controversial *Spartacus*. Unfortunately some members of the public misunderstood the theme which depicted a number of crucifixions. The religious connotation was perhaps too strong for some spectators but it was the performers themselves who suffered the most. Whilst those on the crosses had their hands apparently tied to the crosses, they actually sat on small hidden seats with their legs hanging unsupported. With the exception of one member of the club, all those on the crosses passed out through lack of circulation. The effect was most convincing! One member even needed hospital treatment. Learning from their mistakes, by the time they arrived at North Petherton, the performers had small supports beneath their feet on which to stand.

In 2001 *Mystic Island* almost failed to make it to the Bridgwater Carnival when problems occurred with the generator. By the time the club were ready to pull out, the roads along the procession route were closed and the float had to find a scenic route to get to the line up. The theme depicted four explorers from a museum in search of archaeological treasures on a mysterious island, unaware of the inhabitants who would later be their captors. Best results came at Shepton Mallet and Wells where the club gained fourth places. It was a year which witnessed a marked improvement in the club's performance. In 2002 they presented Disney's *Aladdin*, designed by Jenny Irish, which portrayed the well known story of the poor lad who discovers a magic lamp. Yet again an improvement in standards could be seen. The 2003 entry was *Come to the Circus* which came second in the class of two at Bridgwater but thereafter failed to make the frame. It was a tough year financially for the club and they were only able to produce a very limited entry.

Huckyduck Carnival Club, Shepton Mallet

During the 1970s, the North Somerset village of Coleford held an annual village week, including a small carnival on the Saturday afternoon. The local scouts provided an entry and in 1976 *Pirates* was their theme. The mums and dads created a pirate ship. Of course, even pirate ships must have a name and soon the nickname of the nearby aqueduct was adopted, *Huckyduck*.

Weeks later, the entry was optimistically taken to Frome Carnival. Sadly the heavens opened and the cardboard-built pirate ship collapsed into a soggy mass. To make matters worse, many of the parents of the young scouts, deterred by the appalling weather, failed to turn up to collect their offspring. Those involved in putting on the entry pledged that if they ever again put a carnival float in a procession, it would be for their own entertainment. And thus the Huckyduck Carnival Club was conceived and arrived on the carnival scene the following year with *Bier Fest 77*.

The club at this stage consisted basically of three families. What started out as a walking entry, developed into a mounted entry at Glastonbury Carnival with a single string of lights. 1978 saw the *Sacrifice to the Sun Gods* with several strings of lights and 1979 brought *Guardians of the Dragon* and the club's first entry at Bridgwater Carnival. By 1980 the club had decided to enter as a tableau and has remained as such ever since.

Year by year the club grew stronger, their standards continuously improving. 1983 however was less than successful. The theme of *Gods of Olympus* acquired the nickname of *Gods of the Dark* reflecting the number of power failures the club suffered. 1985 saw a successful entry with the *Smugglers' Inn* which gained second place in the highly competitive open tableaux at Bridgwater and the club was invited to take the float to the Easter Parade in London the following year.

1992's entry – The Greatest Show on Earth.

2002's Runaway Toys.

1992 brought outstanding success albeit tinged with sadness. Keith Watts, a founder member of the club and the cart captain for 1992, sadly passed away just six weeks before Bridgwater Carnival. Nonetheless, the members rallied and produced a float which was a fitting tribute to their lost friend. It proved to be the most popular with the judges around the circuit and the memorable *Greatest Show On Earth* won the County Championship for tableaux for that year. No one could now doubt Huckyduck's credentials as a major league player and the following year's *Dinotopia – A Land Apart from Time* confirmed it, repeating the best tableau in the county experience and only missing out on the overall championship County Cup by half a point, the narrowest possible margin.

In 1994 disaster struck when that year's entry, *Mystical East*, was in a well advanced state. On a Saturday evening fire totally destroyed both the float and the generator. Years of hard work had gone up in flames at the hands, it is suspected, of an arsonist. Quick thinking on the part of Mike Barber and Nick Brixey, two long standing stalwarts of the club, saved the tractor. The following five weeks showed just what carnival and community spirit can achieve. The villagers of Coleford rallied round. Various carnival clubs offered their support in numerous different ways, including the loan of a float. Five weeks after the disaster, the club arrived at Bridgwater and their hard work, often working right through the night, was rewarded with first place in the open tableau class.

In 1997, the club entered with *Showbiz Spectacular*. Ballet dancers, pantomime dames, Can Can girls and even Fred Astaires graced the float. This proved to be the club's most successful year to date with the County Cup taking pride of place in the trophy cabinet. Since that year, Huckyduck have rarely been outside of the top three places anywhere on the circuit. In 1999 they shared third place with *The Hunchback of Notre Dame*. In 2000, *Flamenco Fiesta* shared first place in the tableau class for the county honours and in 2002 they swept the board with *Runaway Toys* with a perfect seven out of seven to share the County Cup with Masqueraders who had similar success in the features class. But success is not only measured in trophies. It can also be measured in the pleasure and satisfaction that the members obtained from their involvement. One way to gauge that is by the number of family members involved. In 2003, Huckyduck could boast three generations all on their entry *Everyone's Favourite Lady*. Christine Watts, a founder member, was there with her daughter Paula, and Paula was there with her eight year old daughter Harriet.

2003's entry was Everyone's Favourite Lady.

King William Carnival Club, Glastonbury

In 1961, two new clubs formed in the Glastonbury area. One was Wick and the other the King William, which took its name from the pub at which they were originally based. Their first entry was a simple affair with *Coates Cider* as their theme. Jars of cider, bales of straw decorated with paper flowers combined with Somerset smocks to provide costumes and props. The members portrayed the role of stereotyped cider drinkers. A generator was borrowed from Street and so short were the club of funds that they manually hauled it all the way from Street to Glastonbury.

Choosing a brand name cider for their theme could have proved a little risky. At the end of the carnival, they returned to their headquarters to be told that representatives from Coates Cider were waiting to meet them. Somewhat nervously they went to face the music. They needn't have worried. The cider company representative was so delighted that he handed over a cheque for £25. It was just the funds that were needed to get the carnival club under way.

Since then the club has taken part in every carnival except one, 1963 when Glastonbury Carnival nearly folded. Throughout that period, Win Clark has been a stalwart member and is the only founder member still with the club. Other stalwarts include Bill Shepard, club chairman and Pat Thick who both joined in 1979. After three or four years of 'anything goes', the club decided to enter a higher class. Wick Carnival Club were going through the same process. It was agreed that Wick would become a feature and King William a tableau, and they have remained thus ever since. Their most successful entry was probably *Swan Fantasy*, an imaginative float which came close to County Cup success but in Glastonbury, at which they needed to clinch first place, and on their home territory, they were awarded a controversial second.

The club which started at the King William, currently resides at the Glastonbury Football Club. At one time they built by the river at Dye House Lane. There was an occasion when early one morning a strong wind raged. Club members were summoned by telephone to get to the building ground as fast as they could. There they saw the wind thrashing the tarpaulin which covered the float. It became obvious that the scaffolding

King William's 2002 Moulin Rouge.

supporting the canvas could take little more punishment and the wind was too strong for the members to attempt to take the tarpaulin off. The only option was to cut the ropes which held the tarpaulin in place. As the last length of rope was cut, the tarpaulin took off and headed straight down the river!

Scaffolding seems to provide occasional problems for the King William club. The year they produced *Tudor Kings and Queens*, they used scaffolding to create the infrastructure for their float. It looked quite good until they reached Bridgwater.

They never quite made the procession. No sooner had they arrived, then the whole scaffolding system collapsed. In more successful years, they have been invited to the Easter Parade, in fact on a number of occasions including 1984 when they took their *Cracker Wonderland* entry. Happy memories remain of those trips during which most of the members went to the metropolis for the weekend, and thoroughly enjoyed themselves. I have yet to discover what happened to the goldfish they caught in the pond of one of the hotels they stayed in!

King William's 2003 entry was Ornamental.

Luckington Carnival Club, Shepton Mallet

In 1979 a carnival club was formed by Kath and Ken Selway, Les Parfitt, his two sons Neil and Allen, and a handful of others. Although some had previously appeared in village carnivals, this was the first time on the big circuit. A quarter of a century later, Ken is president and Les is vice. The club is based at the Royal British Legion in the North Somerset village of Coleford, and as such are neighbours of the Huckyduck Carnival Club. For the first two years the club were known as The Legionnaires, but later changed to the Luckington Carnival Club recognising Luckington Manor Farm, the home of Ken and Kath Selway, on which they build their float.

For their first entry, they chose the theme of *The Mighty Quinn*, a popular record at the time, written by Bob Dylan and recorded by Manfred Mann. On the float were igloos and the younger members of the club were wrapped in sleeping bags and placed inside them. By the time the procession finished, most of those performers were sound asleep.

Luckington has never been a large club but nonetheless has had its moments. In the 1990s they won the County Cup with a *Ship in a Bottle*. On odd occasions, they have broken away from the tableau ranks and performed as a comic feature. One example was *Rafferty's Motor Car* during the performance of which, for some unknown reason, the club members were unable to stop laughing. They also found it hard not to laugh when, after the final carnival at Weston-super-Mare, one of the club members was seen swinging from the curtains of the Winter Gardens as he impersonated Tarzan. His niece Kelly has asked me not to release his name. Kelly Coe is the granddaughter of Ken and Kath Selway and maintains the family tradition, her parents and aunts and uncle all having been involved. Kelly, who for four years was a member of Huckyduck, serves as the club secretary.

Fund raising is perhaps low key compared to some clubs. Jumble sales, dances, bingo, making and selling flower pots, all help to swell the coffers. Their recent entries include 2003's *Clowning Around* and 2004's *Women in Black*.

Luckington Carnival Club Clowning Around *in 2003.*

Pentathlon Carnival Club, North Petherton

One of the most successful tableau clubs on the circuit is North Petherton's Pentathlon Carnival Club based at the Swan Inn. It was in 1971 that the club, then based at the Thatchers Arms at nearby Moorland, first took to the road. Alan Gibbs, the landlord, was one of the team as was Rex Ball, one of the most famous carnival model makers of his era. Their entry *Verdi's Grand Opera Aida* took first place at Bridgwater in the open tableau. It was an amazing achievement for a new club. Thereafter it would be easier to state the years in which they didn't win, such was their string of successes. In their second year, they hit the big time again and were awarded the County Cup for *Ceremonial Procession of India*.

Many clubs, having found a winning formula, consistently re-visit the same theme. Not so Pentathlon. *Scenes From a Bullfight*, *Pride of Scotland* and *The Planet of the Apes* were produced in the next three years, again taking first place honours. It is difficult to think of a greater contrast in choice of themes than in those three entries. They were followed in 1976 by *Fantasy World of the Ice Princess* which, with a string of first places, took the overall county championship, the Starkey Cup.

Pentathlon continued their successful run by taking the county cup on a regular basis: in 1984 with *The Legend of King Arthur,* 1985 with *Star Wars,* then a run of three years starting in 1987 with *The Cossacks, Shogun Lord of the Samurai* and *Cleopatra's Escape from Egypt.* *Enchantica* in 1991 repeated the success. Throughout the 1980s and 1990s even when not winning the County Cup, the club rarely did worse than second place. During this time, their entry of *Hook* gave us a wonderful example of all aspects of stage craft which a tableau needs to produce. The pictures shown demonstrate well the creation of the stage setting, costumes and make up.

1998 *Buffalo Bill's Wild West Show* took first at Bridgwater, North Petherton, and Burnham with second places on the remainder of the circuit. In 1999, *Star Wars – Episode One – the Phantom Menace*

Pentathlon's winning entry for 1998's Buffalo Bill's Wild West Show.

Scenes from Hook *by Pentathlon.*

took the runner up cup in the County Cup challenge and the 2000 entry of *Cavalcade of Carnival* shared first place honours with Huckyduck. 2002 brought *Disney's Heroes and Villains* which was runner up in the tableau class for the County Cup.

The 2003 entry was *Les Miserables* which took first place in the open class tableaux at Bridgwater, where the Wills Carnival Club who had chosen the same theme were in the local class and also took first place.

At the same time, Shambles Carnival Club took third place with *Chitty Chitty Bang Bang*. At North Petherton, Pentathlon took first in the local class but it was not until Burnham that Pentathlon, Wills and Shambles were to all meet head to head. It was to be the Shambles Club's year. They took first place everywhere except Bridgwater. Meanwhile, Wills Carnival Club with the same theme appeared to be just pipping Pentathlon at each carnival except

Shepton Mallet where they pushed Wills into second place (Shambles being local at that venue). It was an unfortunate clash and one that leaves us wondering how the results may have altered if circumstances had been different. Would the judges have viewed the one entry in a better light had a clash not been present? Pentathlon had been beaten into third place overall across the county.

Their most recent entry in 2004 was the imaginative *Lights, Camera, Action* which received disappointing results around the third and fourth spots. It was not Pentathlon's year. Indeed the surprise winner was Gemini with their atmospheric *Pirates of the Caribbean* who the previous year had been a walking entry. Perhaps it served as a wake up call for the county's tableau clubs. And if anyone is likely to respond to the call, Pentathlon could well be the one.

2002's Disney's Heroes and Villains.

Shambles Carnival Club, Shepton Mallet

In 1978 the Shepton Mallet based Fielders Carnival Club took part in its very first carnival. There had previously been a Crown Inn Carnival Club, but when this folded, some of its members re-appeared at the Field Inn. It was from the Fielders Carnival Club that the Shambles Carnival Club took root. 1981 proved a difficult year and the club failed to produce a tableau but instead appeared on foot with a flag-waving *Rule Britannia*. It was not long before a resurrected Fielders bounced back with mostly new members but with their captain Nigel Freeman providing the experience. Martin Dredge eventually took over the captaincy and later became chairman of the club. Problems came in 1985 when

the club was forced to move its headquarters away from the Field Inn. Further problems were added over parking their float at a caravan site. A complaint from the village of Doulting resulted in an enforcement notice being imposed on the club and a disruptive move.

In 1986, the twenty plus members had found a new home at the King's Arms in Shepton Mallet and produced their entry *The Collectors Range of Military Figurines*. 1987 saw the Fielders appear for the first time under their new name – Shambles, with the entry *Martial Arts of the Orient*. By the following year they had moved to the Bell Hotel and more recently settled at the Conservative Club.

2001's Tales of Beatrix Potter.

Fund raising activities have included watering the displays for Shepton in Bloom, working at the Glastonbury Music Festival, the Bath and West Showground, Nunney Street Fayre, car boot sales and many other similar events. In recent years, some memorable entries have been produced including the 1995 *Hocus Pocus* taking advantage of a new cart which gave them the extra length they needed, an entry which brought them seventeen trophies for costumes and tableau pose, originality and art work.

In 1998 *The Flix* was a memorable entry which took third place at Bridgwater, North Petherton, Burnham and Weston with a well deserved first on their home turf at Shepton Mallet. I particularly liked their 2001 entry *Tales of Beatrix Potter*. At home my wife has a collection of the figurines and the reproduction of these on the Shambles float was quite stunning. It was wonderful entry and quite

justified its success in taking the County Cup in the tableau class.

The 2003 entry of *Chitty Chitty Bang Bang* was also notable. A disappointing third place in the open class at Bridgwater was followed by a string of successes. Having dropped two points at Bridgwater, Shambles could only keep their fingers crossed. As the carnivals progressed, Shambles maintained a sequence of five first places. Meanwhile Masqueraders, the rivals for the County Cup, dropped to second place once, and then once more. As the two clubs entered Weston, they were on equal points. It was all to play for. Masqueraders took first place and so did Shambles – but Shambles had tied. In so doing they dropped a half point and missed out on the Starkey Cup as overall champions. It was a fabulous entry which was to earn the Shambles the trophy for best tableau in the procession after narrowly missing out on the overall championship.

Chitty Chitty Bang Bang, *2003*.

Wills Carnival Club

Follow the Yellow Brick Road *of 2001*.

The Wills Carnival Club are currently based at the Great Escape in Bridgwater but have previously been based at both the Blue Boar and more latterly at the Wellworthy Social Club. The club was formed in 1952 by a group of employees from the W. & F. Wills Ltd engineering works. The late Kelvin "Toby" Foster was the longest serving club member and was much respected for his total commitment to carnival. Such was the respect for Toby that on a milestone birthday, the club presented him with a ticket for a flight on Concorde, an aircraft which he greatly admired.

The club's first entry was *Bring 'Em Back Alive* in 1952 which took fourth place in Bridgwater. Four more years of also rans led to eventual success in 1957 with *Life in Arcady*. First place on the road was nearly matched with second place on stage. The next year proved to be even more successful with

Lady Fu-Chen Returns. With first place on stage and road, the club's success continued around the county circuit culminating in the winning of the overall county championship, the Starkey Cup. That success was repeated just a year later with *Boris Godunov*.

Although 1960 and 1961 saw further successes in Bridgwater with nothing less than second on stage or road, the County Cup eluded them. But it was theirs again from 1962 to 1964 with *The Golden Swan*, *Princess Turandot* and *My Lord Mayor*. After a brief spell out of the top spot, Wills returned to win the County Cup once more in 1971 with *Death or Glory Boys*. This particular entry is still remembered as a classic. Depicting the *Charge of the Light Brigade*, the model horses were particularly memorable. Never before had such fine replicas been seen in the carnival circuit. But it wasn't just the horses, it was

2003's Les Miserables.

the whole portrayal of the folly and the glory of that famous event. The horses were so good that the following year they appeared again on the float of another club, and then again and again. My memory fails me here and I confess I am unable to remember the detail but carnival legend now has it that they remain the only horses to complete the carnival circuit on six different occasions.

The Wills Carnival Club had set new standards and around them other clubs took great leaps forward with their presentations. Despite first place in Bridgwater in 1972 with *Scenes from Aladdin*, the club went through a less successful spell through the 70s and 80s. The early part of the 70s saw the Town Council Carnival Club making their mark as standards continued to improve, and then from the mid 70s and through the 80s it was the newcomer Bohemians Carnival Club who set the pace. A momentary return to the top spot in 1980 with *Holiday on Ice* was the only moment of promise for the Wills Club until 1987.

1987 and 1988 brought the club back to their first place spot with *Phantom of the Opera* and *Solomon and Sheba*. After slipping to second place with *Starlight Express* in 1989, Wills produced a series of first place winners, increasingly and successfully choosing West End shows as their themes. *Phantom of the Opera, Starlight Express, Barnum* and *Cats* serve as examples. These also brought a string of first places on the stage although it has to be said that the opposition on stage was weakening. But Wills are not a club to let the grass grow under their feet and they had sufficient imagination to introduce new techniques to the stage. Rather than have the curtains close between their various scenes whilst performers and props were moved around, they left the curtain open and dropped the stage lights so that the faint outline of the movement was visible but the audience no longer viewed a blank curtain. The use of a momentary flash of light was another introduced technique, as was dry ice smoke effect, previously unseen in tableau presentations.

The wonderfully imaginative 1994 entry of *Toys and Dolls* did the double with stage and road success and also brought the County Cup back to Wills Carnival Club's trophy cabinet. Likewise *Silverball Mania*, a depiction of a pinball machine and using the music Pinball Wizard from the rock opera Tommy, maintained the County Cup.

In recent years among the most memorable entries have been 1998's *Beauty and the Beast* with its exceptionally fine models, *Moulin Rouge* and *Les Miserables*, all following the themes of West End block-busting stage shows. *Beauty and the Beast* took first place at Bridgwater and North Petherton. But at Burnham, the first time it came head to head with Pentathlon's *Buffalo Bill's Wild West Show*, it was pipped into second place. Thereafter it was first place all the way and the cup for the best tableau across the county. That year the costumes were quite stunning and well deserved to take the costume cups at so many carnivals.

The choice of *Les Miserables* for 2003 was perhaps unfortunate in that it clashed in the same year with Pentathlon's entry with the same theme title. The two were so similar that it may well have influenced the judges attitudes allowing Shambles to take a consistent run of first places.

Over the years, Wills Carnival Club have produced more than just their winning entries. On an annual basis, the Bridgwater carnival clubs have produced an Old Folks Show, a charitable and well attended concert for the elderly. Members of Wills Carnival Club have been at the forefront when producing that show especially in the organising of the scores of raffle prizes and working back stage.

Wills 2004 Aegyptus.

THE COMIC FEATURES

Newmarket Carnival Club

You don't have to be mad to be in carnival but you do have to be at least slightly mad to be in a comic feature and this is especially true of the Newmarket Carnival Club. The club was founded in 1977 by extroverts such as Geoff Paisey and Keiron Howes. Keiron, a former member of the Renegades Carnival Club, remains with the club to this day and more than a quarter of a century later can still be seen taking part in the whacky portrayals at which this club is such a master. The late Geoff Paisey was another such character. On one occasion, Geoff was swinging wildly on a rope at the back of the float whilst in procession. Unfortunately he went too far, came off the rope and was run over by the generator. It could have been fatal for a less fit person,

Geoff had been a high standard rugby player, but for Geoff it was serious crush injuries which kept him out of action for some while.

The Newmarket Carnival Club have perhaps had more than their share of injuries. At Weston Carnival when the club's theme was *Sex Bomb*, club stalwart Sue Duddridge was performing dressed as a cavalier. As the float passed along the Boulevard, with the voice of Tom Jones rendering 'Sex Bomb', a decorative revolving wheel stopped spinning and headed straight for Sue. Catching sight of the missile heading towards her, Sue leapt from the cart to avoid being a casualty of the offending wheel. Nonetheless, Sue was knocked unconscious and onlookers watched as her husband Barry, a leading

2003 and Sisters Are Doing It For Themselves.

Carnival extrovert Keiron Howes gives his interpretation of Flash Gordon above and on the right thinks he is Shirley Bassey!

light and key member in the club, put Sue into the recovery position. Five minutes later, this true performer had recovered and was back on the float performing – with the wheel safely secured by the club engineers. Their reward was a third place on the night and second place overall for the comic feature's county cup.

For the Newmarket success first came in 1984 with *Finger Lickin Chickens*. Then in 1988 came *Hey*

Big Spender which proved to be the first of a series of first places for the club. The 2003 entry was *Sisters are Doing It For Themselves* which took first place in Bridgwater. Their success continued across the county bringing them the County Cup in the comic feature class. That success was repeated in 2004 with *High*, where frilly knickers and waving skirts reflected the imagination of Young Farmer entries of a generation ago.

Highbridge Young Farmers Carnival Club

For many years Young Farmers' carnival entries were predictable in their style of presentation. If the performers used bales of hay as props, wore Wellingtons and smocks, had cider jars festooning the floor, waved wet fish around on the end of a fishing line and generally did not know what to do other than chase each other around the cart, then it was a Young Farmers entry. Thank goodness they are getting better as shown by the 2003 Highbridge Young Farmers' entry of *Get off my Land* which depicted hippy travellers with a 'love bus' at one end of the float with angry farmers at the other. This earned an uncontested first place at their home carnival at Burnham and higher single figures around the rest of the circuit.

Based at the Coopers Arms in Highbridge, the club has a membership between the ages of thirteen and twenty-six. Their recent previous entries in the comic classes include *Rain Men, Get Off My Land* and *Barbie Dolls*.

In 2003 Highbridge Young Farmers ask the public to 'Get off my Land'.

FEATURES ON FOOT

Wilfs Carnival Club

1991's Wilfs' Synchronised Swimming.

The Wilfs Carnival Club is infamous around the county circuit for its occasional moments of absolute brilliance. The comic walking feature spun off from the British Flag Carnival Club. Local legend has it that after an internal rift, a group of the older members decided 'We Immediately Left Flag' and hence became the Wilfs. Their first entry in 1989 was *Betty Woods Former Formation Dance Team*. Bett Woods is herself something of a carnival legend and choreographed the British Flag for more years than I can remember. Indeed she had helped many a club during the Trojan years of service she has given to carnival. But back to the Wilfs.

I have always felt that comedy is the most difficult art form to portray in carnival. A good idea on the drawing board may go flat in front of an audience. There is no way of predicting the impact of a theme. But in 1991 the Wilfs produced a classic – *Wilfs Synchronised Swimming Display*. Now synchronised swimming has always been an entirely female domain. It is the only Olympic sport in which men are not allowed to compete. The Wilfs, hairy men every one of them, introduced synchronised swimming to carnival. A huge blue plastic sheet was fitted over a wooden frame on wheels such that the blue sheet appeared as the surface of a swimming pool some four feet off the ground. In the sheet, holes were cut through which the 'swimmers' rose to surface with their nose pinchers in place and one arm raised. In synchronised fashion, they slowly rose and then gracefully sank. Then up through each hole came a leg and slowly sank. The effect was wonderful and had the spectators in fits of laughter everywhere. It must surely remain the most effective piece of comedy ever produced in a carnival procession. Needless to say it took a string of first places on the circuit.

In 1994 with the opening of the channel tunnel, the Wilfs produced *Le Tunnel de Change* with a mobile tunnel into which they entered as Englishmen to emerge as French at the other end.

The following year they were hairy Scots as *Mac Wilfs & Their Hunt for Nessie*. In 1998 if length of title had any influence on the results, the Wilfs should have done much better with *Wilfs Present Basil Flatley and the Bridgwater River Parrett Dancers Direct From Broadway!*

They continue to produce entertaining ideas at relatively low cost which is quite important to them. By keeping it simple, they can enjoy the pleasures of carnival without the trauma of huge fund-raising projects and without the pain of unrelenting hours spent building a carnival float as they experienced in their days as members of British Flag. It's a most satisfying way of having your cake and eating it, of retiring yet still taking part.

2003. A Day out with the Wilfs.

THE JUVENILE CLUBS

Hillview Juvenile Carnival Club from Burnham-on-Sea presented Flying Circus *in 2003.*

The **Key Kids Carnival Club** are based at Meare near Glastonbury. In fact they share the Countryman Inn with the Masqueraders Carnival Club as their headquarters. Little wonder then that the enormous cartoon character models shown below on the Key Kids *Looney Tunes* were first seen on Masqueraders float just three years before.

Marina Sydenham, Bridgwater's premiere juvenile club, was founded in 1966 as the Marina Row Carnival Club and with that origin can claim to be the longest running of our juvenile clubs. Originally based around the Marina Row area of the town, they later merged with the Sydenham JCC to become Marina Sydenham around 1975. There successes in the juvenile mounted category have been considerable. In recent year they have captured the County Cup for juveniles in 2001 with *Top'n Tails*, in 2002 with *Intergalactic Circus* and in 2003 with *Grease*. In 2004, they slipped into a consistent second place with their *Rio Ritmo*, being pipped at the post by the **Toppers Juvenile Carnival Club of North Petherton** with their entry *Luck of the Irish*. Their earlier entries included *Minstrel Showtime*, *Apprenticeship* and *Octopuses Garden*.

Marina Sydenham Juvenile Carnival Club presented Grease *in 2003.*

Toppers Juvenile Carnival Club of North Petherton presented Octopuses Garden *in 2003.*

CLUBS FROM THE WESSEX GRAND PRIX CIRCUIT

The Wessex Grand Prix Circuit spans the three counties of Dorset, Somerset and Wiltshire and covers Sturminster Newton, Trowbridge, Mere, Frome, Shaftesbury, Gillingham plus Castle Cary and Ansford. Whilst these carnivals are smaller than their Somerset County Circuit neighbours, they have their own character and charm. By way of example, Gillingham carnival procession includes a parade of steam engines which precedes the carnival entries and at the rear of the procession is a parade of steam driven lorries. Such entries add both interest and charm to these Wessex carnivals and are items not seen at the 'Magnificent Seven'. The Wessex Circuit also provides many of the entries which go on to take part in the major processions and add greatly to the spectacle.

For many years, the **Aliens** competed as a walking entry. The club started as a family group. Membership grew with people joining from Chippenham, Westbury and Warminster. Recent presentations from this Frome-based feature included *Mesheeca*, their year 2000 walking entry which almost swept the board on the Wessex Circuit; indeed they had twelve firsts across sixteen carnivals.

In 2001 they produced their first mounted entry with *Dancin'*. 2002's *Imhotep* took another first at Warminster, success which was repeated in 2003 with *Cinders* Whilst gaining good results at their home circuit carnivals, they have been less successful when competing against the larger clubs on the Somerset County Circuit albeit a ninth place at Bridgwater in 2003 must be considered a good result.

As the clock approached midnight, Aliens presented Cinders *in 2003.*

Britannia Carnival Club's 2003 entry Voodooby Doo.

Hot Rock Carnival Club's 2003 entry took them Dancin' Tonite.

Revellers' 2003 entry was Samba.

Britannia Carnival Club are based at Castle Cary. Their 2003 entry was *Voodooby Doo*. They managed sixth at Bridgwater where they were not up against the Bridgwater clubs and seventeenth at Burnham.

Hot Rock are one of the most successful Wessex clubs. In recent years, their entries of *Voodoo Poison*, *Trick or Treat*, *Brasil*, *Dancing Tonite* and many others have brought a string of first prizes on their home circuit. Moving on to the main Somerset circuit their results slip as they come up against the larger clubs. But even on their home circuit, the competition is tough and a string of first places in preceding years is no guarantee of continued success. In 2004, their entry of *Arcadia* was just pipped to the post by their local rivals the Revellers.

Based at Motcombe near Shaftesbury, the **Revellers Carnival Club** has been one of the more successful on the Wessex Circuit. Recent years have seen a string of runner up awards with Hot Rock

taking the glory but by 2004 the tables seemed to be turning as Revellers picked up a series of first places on the Wessex Circuit with their entry of *Pirates*.

Long gone are the days when carnival clubs begged, borrowed or stole (allegedly) almost everything for their floats. The **Chameleon Carnival Club** of Frome in their time were among the best of them. When a considerable quantity of scaffolding tubing was required one year, and members of the club had heard about a large quantity of disused boiler tubes apparently going to waste, a midnight raid was organised. Two tonnes of useful tubing was acquired. Unfortunately everyone involved was covered in black, the lorry was covered in black and the yard in which the tubes were stored was covered in black. The following evening, the loss of two tonnes of tubing from a Bristol site was reported on Police Five. When pampas grass was required to enhance the performance of *Cleopatra's Barge*, a large house in Frome became the target. It had one of the largest beds of pampas grass the county had seen. Under cover of darkness, a club member, who in the interest of anonymity we shall refer to simply as 'The Turk', stealthily crept into the centre of the pampas grass and cut as much as was required. The following morning, viewed from the outside, the decorative pampas appeared untouched. Viewed from a high up bedroom window, there was a gaping hole and an unseasonable crop circle!

A fund-raising venture also made the headline when the *News of the World* reported 'Village Hall sees sex show as fund raiser for local charity!' But perhaps their gravest offence was when they presented their *Grandmaster Chess Set*, where a giant chess set was portrayed in green and white. It was wonderfully effective and greatly enhanced by the use of green and white quartz chipping, the kind found in graveyards!

The Chameleon Carnival Club have probably experienced the highs and lows of carnival more than most clubs. At times, they have produced brilliant entries which have swept the board and taken the overall County Cup with such entries as the classic *Grandmaster Chess Set* in 1975 and *England Expects (Death of Nelson)* in 1983. At other times they have struggled and in recent years have appeared more frequently as a comic feature. In 2001 it was *Bob the Builder* and in 2002 they appeared with a much reduced float. It was just a week before their first carnival that their pub headquarters closed and they were unable to finish their windmill centre piece for their entry of *Truth, Beauty, Freedom and Love*. The windmill was completed but was a fraction of the intended size. But they bounced back. 2003 gave us *Belle Bottoms and Busty Boys*. This is a club which will bounce back and one which I long to see producing those memorable tableau floats for which they were so respected in earlier years.

In 1983 Chameleons presented England Expects (Death of Nelson).

In 2003, the Oasis Carnival Club presented Amethyst.

The Oasis Carnival Club are based at the Old Globe in Frome and appear on the Wessex Circuit and Somerset County Carnival circuit as a tableau, and with some very credible entries to their name. They are quite used to success on the Wessex Circuit and when competing against the very best on the county circuit, will typically feature around the fifth to eighth slots, which is highly praiseworthy for any club in this extremely competitive field.

In 2001 they presented *Neptune's Fantasy* and the following year *Disney*. I suspect it was this latter entry which led to a website referring to the trial by club members of one of their gang for the aggravated assault of Pinocchio on the night of North Petherton Carnival. It seems that at North Petherton, Trevor Knight accidentally collided with the model of Pinocchio and caused limited damage. The case against Trevor was presented in

such a way that he 'approached Pinocchio from the rear and wrestled him to the ground' and consequently broke his legs, removed his hands and allegedly then demonstrated fake sympathy as a crowd of onlookers watched his attempts to re-assemble the dismembered puppet.

When Pinocchio, who was clearly not having a good carnival season, fell off the float after Weston carnival, it was claimed by certain club members that Pinocchio was so traumatised by the experience at North Petherton that he feared for his safety on the trip back to Frome. It is alleged that this puppet was seen to be unsuccessfully trying to hitch a lift from another carnival float when his hand fell off. Unable now to hitch a lift, he leapt from the float and decapitated himself. The last I heard was that Trevor Knight was appealing for character witnesses and the club had sent condolences to Pinocchio's family in Collodi.

Cary Comedians Carnival Club was founded in 1977 and is one of the county's well established comic feature clubs. Their success has been rewarded in 1998 and 2001 with the County Cup for Comic Features. The 2003 *Snow Joke* came second at Bridgwater and across the county they took second place to Newmarket for the comic feature county cup.

Cary Comedian's 2003 entry – Snow Joke.

CLUBS FROM THE SOUTH SOMERSET CIRCUIT

Club 2000's Space Balls.

Club 2000 are based at Chard. *Castles in the Air,* their 2002 entry was followed by *Space Balls* in 2003. First place at Yeovil, second at Ilminster reflected their success around the smaller circuits. *Space Ball* came twentieth at Bridgwater when it met the large open field of features from across the county. Their 2004 entry *Run for your Life* achieved similar results.

Domino Carnival Club is one of the longer established clubs in the South Somerset group and has produced good standard floats for decades. In 2001 they produced *Spirit of Afrika* in 2001, *Vegas* in 2002 and *Sunlords in 2003*.

The **DT6 Carnival Club** comes from Bridport in Dorset but compete on the South Somerset and Somerset County Circuits. They have tremendous fun as a comic feature with themes like *Abba Nice Day* in 2001, *Chocoholics* in 2002, whilst 2003 brought *Whose house is it anyway?* which collected a number of first places around the minor circuits.

Domino's 2003 entry was Sunlords.

Whose House Is It Anyway? *was the question asked by DT6 in 2003.*

Gemini Carnival Club of Ilminster started life as two clubs. Aldon Vale Carnival Club was founded by Ray Blackmore and Bob Hurlestone around 1960. The club used to change between tableau and feature in alternate years until settling as a feature. In 1997 the Springfield Carnival Club and Aldon Vale Carnival Club were both finding survival in carnival tough going. It was soon realised the future of the clubs lay in combining as one and the Gemini Carnival Club was founded and Ray Blackmore serves as its president. Since then the club has had its ups and downs. Recent entries included *Hellfire* which took overall first place on the South Somerset Circuit and took a very satisfactory fourth place in the open features at Bridgwater. By 2003 the club were struggling again, financially, and appeared as a walking feature with *The Red Barrows*. By 2004, they were able to afford to put a float on the road but lacked the funds to build a feature float. Mike Newbury put forward the idea of *Pirates of the Caribbean* as something that was simple enough to be able to afford. The original thinking was to have a galleon with a harbourside at the back. As the float progressed, the idea of the harbour was dropped and the club stuck to the galleon. Having completed the South Somerset Circuit, they were delighted to have taken first place at each carnival. Then came Bridgwater. To their delight, they took first place again, albeit not competing against the likes of the Wills club who were in the local class. Then at North Petherton, they beat all the other tableaux. The club now had just one carnival to go, Glastonbury. They had not entered for the rest of the circuit, having no idea how successful they were going to be. At the 'Black Sabbath' celebrations, members of the club were persuaded to go for the County Cup. A rapid series of phone calls to the conveners of the other carnivals resulted in their belated, but welcome, entries being accepted. The rest is history. The club completed a clean sweep of first prizes and gained the overall carnival championship.

Inevitably controversy loomed in the wake of their success. Questions were raised regarding the late entries. Should they or should they not have been accepted? Each carnival has a closure date for

2004's awesome entry from Gemini Carnival Club – Pirates of the Caribbean.

entries. Does this mean that all the clubs can put their entries in late? The questions continue. It's a valid argument but equally a great shame that it needed to be raised and in so doing detract from a wonderful moment of glory.

The burning question now is 'How do they follow that?' Deep down, they wanted to be a feature. In 2003, it was lack of finances which obliged them to appear as a walking entry. In 2004, they wanted to be a feature but could only afford to appear as a tableau, there not being the need to spend large sums on motors and the like. But the tableau brought the ultimate success. So do they continue as a tableau having had a taste of success or do they produce a feature entry? Only time will tell.

One of the strongest clubs on the South Somerset circuit is **Harlequin Carnival Club** of Ilminster. Their 1998 entry *The New Starlight Express* took second at Bridgwater and a third at Glastonbury proving that South Somerset can compete in the premier league. In 2001 they took first place in the walking groups of adult masquer-

aders with *Circus of Wonder*. 2002 produced *Mardi Gras* and in 2003 it was *Fantasmic* which was outstanding on its own circuit with credible results on the county circuit such as second at Bridgwater and sixth at Burnham

In 2004 the club produced the excellent *Yuan Xiao Jie* which having taken third place at Wellington, took first prizes all around the South Somerset Circuit to become the South Somerset overall feature winner. With second, fourth and third at Bridgwater, North Petherton and Burnham, the club looked well set for some promising results. Sadly generator failure excluded them from the rest of the circuit and we must wait to see what the future brings for this club which shows such promise.

One Plus One Carnival Club are based at Ilminster. This comic feature club produced *Chitty Chitty Bang Bang* in 2003 which took best music at Chard, second in the comic class and with similar results around the South Somerset Circuit. It also took a well deserved third place at Bridgwater.

In 2003 Harlequin Carnival Club produced Fantasmic.

One Plus One's Chitty Chitty Bang Bang.

The Poppe Inne's 2003 entry was SK8R BOI.

The **Poppe Inne Carnival Club** was formed in 1985 and is based at the Poppe Inne, Tatworth where they produce their comic entries. It is an interesting pub for a headquarters and somewhat unusual in having an annual 'candle auction'. The club has a busy year taking part in the Devon, South Somerset and Somerset County Circuits. In 2004 they had a most successful year with a tremendous run of first places, sufficient for them easily to win both the South and East Devon and the South Somerset overall championships in the comic cate-

gory with their entry of *Shooter*.

Recent years have seen a steady improvement in the standard of tableau entries from the **St Peters Carnival Club** of Yeovil. Their 2000 entry of *Excalibur* hit the number six spot at Bridgwater. In 2003 their entry was *Lambeth* which achieved fourth place at Bridgwater and similar results around the circuit. Their *Victorian Christmas* entry for 2004 achieved many first prizes in their local circuits and maintained middle order positions on the Somerset County Circuit.

St Peters 2003 entry was Lambeth.

CLUBS FROM THE DEVON CIRCUITS

High Spirits, Honiton

East Devon's newest club is the Honiton based High Spirits. With members ranging from fourteen years old to sixty five, they can boast a membership of around forty. They claim their objective as a club is to enter as many carnivals and have as much fun as possible. It's the true spirit of carnival. Their season starts early with Seaton, Axminster and Sidmouth Carnivals among the many on their agenda. From the Devon Circuit, they move on to South Somerset and then join the Somerset County circuit. It's a long season for these Devon clubs.

Their 2003 entry of *A Load of Looneys* took second place at Exmouth and eighteenth at Bridgwater. Such a range in results reflects not only on how the standard improves dramatically as the season progresses but on how High Spirits put taking part before the glory.

High Spirits provided A Load of Looneys *in 2003.*

Phoenix Carnival Club, Honiton

A relatively new club to the Devon Circuit, the Phoenix Carnival Club are also based at Honiton in Devon. Theirs is a long season, attending eleven carnivals in Devon, then Wellington and Taunton before joining the major Somerset County Circuit.

Formed as recently as 1995, they have a young membership supported by a few more experienced stalwarts. Their 2003 entry was *Nataraja* which took first place at Exmouth Carnival, fourteenth at Burnham and twenty-first at Bridgwater.

Phoenix provided a Vampire Wedding *in 2004.*

Sidvale Carnival Club, Sidmouth

Sid Vale completes the list of my selected Devon clubs and again it is worth stressing the commitment of these Devon clubs to carnival. They may not be the biggest but they certainly show the greatest stamina. With their carnival season starting during the summer months, they then appear at a carnival somewhere every Saturday until they join the November processions. Whilst the big clubs can boast having appeared in seven carnivals, these Devon lads and lasses will have appeared in almost twenty by the time they take their well earned winter break. Any club treasurer will appreciate the cost of traveling; diesel, generator hire, insurance, tractor hire, coaches, et cetera. That inevitably places a huge burden on the clubs to raise sufficient funds to complete their itinerary. Well done, Devon.

Sidvale's 2003 entry in the feature class was Kung Hei Fat Choi.

CLUBS FROM THE INDEPENDENT CIRCUITS

Merlins Carnival Club, Barton St David

The Merlins Carnival Club are based at Barton St David and Keinton Mandeville and build their float at nearby Parbrook village. In 1997 the club took a break when they moved sites but bounced back in 1998 to produce *Spirit of Arabia*. In more recent years they have produced *Joseph*, *100 Years of Disney*, *Divali Nights* and *Voodoo*.

2003's Divali Nights *from the Merlins Carnival Club.*

Oscars Carnival Club, Crewkerne

The Oscars comic feature are based at Oscars Wine Bar in Crewkerne and appear on the South Somerset and Somerset County Circuits. Their 2003 entry *Oliver Twisted* picked up the prize for best art work at Yeovil and came ninth in the open comic features class at Bridgwater. In 2004 *Oz-cars* maintained middle order positions in the comic feature classes around the county.

Oliver Twisted from 2003.

Prattens Carnival Club, Midsomer Norton

Prattens Carnival Club are based at Midsomer Norton where they are the premier feature club. The club was founded in 1979 and is based at the Prattens Westfield Amateur Sports and Social Club. They can boast in excess of thirty members.

Pratten's 2003 entry was Aquario.

Waterside Carnival Club, Midsomer Norton

Waterside Carnival Club, whose headquarters are at the Welton Rovers Football Club at Midsomer Norton, was formed in 1975. The original members were employees of the former St Peter's Clarks' Shoe Factory who formed a juvenile club. Midsomer Norton Carnival had not been held for some fifteen years and the creation of the Waterside Club coincided with the return of the local carnival. In later years the club changed to the comic feature class. Their 2004 entry of *Peckham's Plonkers*, based on the TV series 'Only Fools and Horses' was well received around the county circuit.

Waterside Carnival Club's Robots *of 2003*.

BYGONE CLUBS

There have of course been numerous clubs which have come and gone, far too many to include in this volume. And so I concentrate my efforts on some of those worthy of inclusion for their uniqueness or outstanding achievements. From a personal point of view, although I am a feature man myself, I view with particular sadness the loss of tableau clubs. At the time of writing, Bridgwater has only two surviving. These tableaux were the origins of our carnival and if for no other reason than that it is sad to see them diminish.

Bohemians Carnival Club

One of Bridgwater's most successful tableau clubs in its time were the Bohemians who started life as the Hinkley Point Carnival Club and changed their name in 1980. In existence from 1967 to 1994 they produced dozens of outstanding entries during their relatively brief spell. Their 1967 entry of *Cleopatra – Queen of Egypt* took first place in the open tableau at the first attempt. The following year they were part of the Bridgwater Gangs and Features and competing as a Bridgwater local club. With themes ranging from *Ivan the Terrible* to the *Butterfly Ball*, from 1968 to 1975 they were knocking on the door of success on the road whilst picking up a string of first prizes in the stage shows. Then came the 1976 *Samurai*, 1977's

Carneval Venezia – *Bohemian Carnival Club's entry in 1989.*

King Ludwig's Journey of Fantasy, 1978's *History of Capo-di-Monte* and 1979's *Regimental Glory* which brought them four successive years of first places. Three times in that period they were invited to perform at the London Easter Parade. *King Ludwig's Journey of Fantasy* and *History of Capo-di-Monte* provided excellent examples of the model maker's craft and there are few that would argue that Bohemian's David Faulks remains one of the most talented of all time.

In the years that followed up to 1994, six more first places were achieved at Bridgwater, including another string of four in succession. Numerous first places were also achieved during those years on the stage, including the Walter Hooper Cup as overall champions in 1979 and 1990.

The Bohemians Carnival Club, based at the Quantock Gateway, did much in its time to push forward the standards of tableau presentation and its disappearance was a great loss. Their success around the county brought them overall county championship honours in 1974, 1977, 1979 and 1981 with the best tableau award in 1968 and 1980. That's some record for a club with a history of only twenty seven years. Unfortunately lack of funds and lack of members brought their demise after the 1994 carnival.

Cardiff Arms / Pig and Whistle / Pariah Carnival Club

There are few clubs which change their discipline from feature to tableau or vice versa. But that was achieved by the club which began life as the Cardiff Arms feature and finished life as Pariah and a tableau. The Cardiff Arms, a Bridgwater West Street pub, introduced a carnival club in 1937 with Harry Crocker and Len Rawles as founder members. Whilst there is no record which details their success or otherwise on the road, they managed to take first place on the stage with *Gentlemen of Old England*, success which they repeated the following year with *Harmonica Minstrels*. There then followed a succession of also rans with one second place.

In 1955 they appeared as the *Eastern Fantasies* in a performance which I remember quite clearly. My mother was the dressmaker and having appeared the year before with the Hope Inn Carnival Club, I was considered suitable material to appear on stage and road as a slave boy. I was just eight years old. From where I stood at the back of the float, I could see everything going on along the length of the float. This included watching one of the club members high up on a flying carpet. During the Bridgwater procession, a mindless individual in the crowd deemed it amusing to throw a lighted firework onto the flying carpet. The danger was obvious. The punishment was swift. One of the Manley brothers leapt off the float, let swing with one hell of a punch, and the offender buckled to the ground. The Manley brother promptly leapt back onto the float and continued as if nothing had happened. The next memorable night came at Shepton Mallet Carnival on a bitterly cold evening. My mother was a member of the Methodist Church and so was against alcohol, and clearly at eight years old, I was not going to get any. Or so she thought. Two ladies on the float, who knew how to keep warm, each plied me with a drop of something to keep the chill out, unaware that they were not the only one doing so. Each of them whispered 'Don't tell Mum!' I don't remember the rest of the evening and I'm sure I should have since it was so cold.

The following year, they acquired their first trophy. It was first place at Midsomer Norton with *The Southerners*, a depiction of the American Civil War. The following year, 1957, they took second place in Bridgwater with *Down on the Caribbean*, with a third place on stage. It was to be their best year. Results improved as they travelled around the county in a year in which they were awarded the County Cup, their first and only real success.

In 1965 they reformed at the Pig and Whistle, taking the name of the pub for the club name. Fred Villis, the landlord, had been a member of the club during the years at the now closed Cardiff Arms. From then until 1986 they appeared as a feature club but were never to repeat their earlier successes. In 1987 they appeared for the first time as Pariah Carnival Club having crossed the line to become a tableau. Apart from twice achieving first on stage, they never quite made the break through to success, achieving seconds, thirds and fourths in a class of just four competitors. By 1996 they had disbanded and Bridgwater was left with one fewer tableau.

Cardiff Arms Carnival Club's 1955 entry was **Eastern Fantasies.** *The author is present, aged eight, as a slave boy.*

Pariah's 1992 stage show – Quest for Merlin.

Pariah Carnival Club presented the Quest for Merlin *in 1992.*

Suffragettes Carnival Club

One of the most noteworthy of the bygone clubs has to be the Suffragettes. It was all down to Daphne Richards and a group of friends who decided to produce an all female club. 1967 saw their first entry with *Votes for Women*, what else could they have done! With eighth on the road and sixth on the stage it was a credible first entry. *Festival of the Spanish Gypsies* was followed by *London Pride*. Six more appearances took them up to 1974 and their final appearance in *Country Style*. From 1970 onwards they never managed to lift themselves out of the lower order positions. The ultimate demise was in part down to the higher turn over of members experienced in girl groups. During their years, their headquarters had been the Three Crowns and the Rose and Crown, both in Bridgwater's St Mary Street.

They were not the first all female club to take part. In the late nineteenth century, there was a special class for Female Gangs and in 1934 the Quantock Preserving Company produced an all female entry. The closest we have today to an all female club is ironically the YMCA Club!

Some of the others

Most Bridgwater pubs at some time or another have had a carnival club based at their premises. A list of bygone clubs reads like a list of bygone pubs: Bakers Arms, Bird In Hand, Black Horse, Blake Arms, Bristol and Exeter, Cardiff Arms, Clarence Tap (a bar at the rear of the Royal Clarence), Cottage Inn, Crown, Devonshire Arms, Dolphin, Golden Ball, Golden Lion, Green Dragon, Hope and Anchor, Hope Inn, Malt Shovel, Market House, North Pole, Rose and Crown, Ship Afloat, Steam Packet, Three Crowns, White Hart and the White Lion. Each of these once had a club and most of these inns are now long gone.

Then there comes the list of factory or work based clubs: British Cellophane, Coated Fencing, Cryptonians, Hardy Spicer, Kraft, Quantock Preserving Co., Railway, Somerset Trading Co., Starkey Knight & Ford, Town Council Employees, Wellworthys, Wilkinson & Lengs and Wilmot Breedons. To read such lists almost suggests that carnival is in decline but far from it. There are more entries today than ever before and they just keep getting better.

PART 9

The Future

Policing

1989 was a turning point for carnivals across the county in the way that events were policed and marshalled. In April 1989, 93 football supporters were killed in Britain's worst ever sporting event disaster. It was at the Hillsborough ground in Sheffield when Nottingham Forest were playing Liverpool in the semi-final of the FA Cup. The stand at the Leppings Lane end of the ground was filled beyond capacity. Outside the ground, 2000 Liverpool supporters were waiting to get in. Police, believing that those outside the ground were at risk of being crushed and that instructions had been received to open the gates, did so and let them in. As the fans rushed forward, those inside were forced against the high security fences, many killed by the crush.

The police were severely criticised for their actions and since Hillsborough have taken a very different role when policing major public events. Historically, the police helped to marshall the crowds and traffic. But in the light of the Hillsborough experience, they now attend only to deal with crime and the responsibility for crowd control has passed to the organising carnival committees.

At the same time, in Bridgwater the local police chief, Superintendent Colin Turnbull was arguing that the local authority should provide an additional 100 crowd control barriers. He claimed that 'lager louts' were throwing coins and beer at his officers. Sedgemoor District Council's Chief Executive, David Tremlett, responded by stating that the police should have arrested far more than the eleven miscreants they had taken into custody. Turnbull's response was that because of the threat of crowd surge, he could not take officers away from those vulnerable positions. Inevitably policing numbers were reduced and marshalling from volunteers increased in order to compensate. In recent years it has been quite noticeable how the quantity and quality of marshals has improved and Bridgwater College even offers training for event stewards and marshals.

Threats to the future

The views expressed here are very much my own opinion but based on a lifetime's experience of carnival. If there are any threats to the future of carnival, I believe they will come from acts of disorder and the implications of insurance premiums against a background of extortionate litigation claims, albeit probably not related to carnivals per se.

To deal first with acts of disorder. Our carnivals are notorious as family events. The crowds are good natured, covering the full range of ages and social groups. Crowd disorder is rare but when it does happen, it comes outside of those pubs frequented by the younger fraternity.   In the Cornish town of Padstow, where they celebrate May Day with the Hobby Horse processing through the streets, the event became too popular for its own good. Heavy drinking during the day by those who had nothing to do with the celebration itself, had led to an unacceptable level of public disorder and the future of the historic event came under threat. The locals, in order to regain control, campaigned for all pubs to close on the day of the event. Even the supermarkets were persuaded not to sell alcohol. Good order was restored and the tradition continues. But it acts as a cautionary reminder of how those mindless minorities who have nothing to do with the event itself can bring its very existence under threat.

At the Somerset carnivals, there is no control over who comes to spectate. There are no admission gates and the good will of those present is relied upon to maintain good order. The carnivals survive in part because of that good will.

The other concern is that of insurance premiums. Events such as our carnivals cannot go ahead without insurance cover. The organisers are in the hands of the insurance companies. Today we can read on a daily basis of huge insurance claims being made against organisations by individuals. It would only take one massive claim at someone else's event, the Notting Hill Carnival, the Grand National, a cup final, anything, and insurance companies could well change their attitude towards the risk of major public events such as our carnivals. If such a change put insurance premiums beyond reach, there may be few individuals prepared to get involved with such expensive risks. Likewise if, as the result of an unforeseen disaster, one of the band of organisers was taken to court, perhaps for corporate negligence, what would be the impact on the band of enthusiastic volunteers who keep our traditions alive?

If however, such risks are managed, then there is no reason why our traditional celebrations should

157

not continue for another 400 years. It will have to evolve. It will have to keep up with the times. Thus far it has done an extremely good job of doing just that and there is no reason to believe it will not continue. But look at how forms of entertainment have changed in just fifty years. Television has revolutionised the entertainment industry and people's expectations change continuously. However, those in the carnival communities have always shown tremendous flair and adaptability. They possess all the attributes to ensure a long and prosperous future for our carnival performers. But it will only happen if the committees and the clubs are given the licence to evolve the events to keep pace with the times whilst maintaining the traditional character which gives the carnivals their uniqueness.

Increasing the effectiveness

The one area which remains weak is in collecting money from the viewing public. Collectors with tins and collecting floats are used to encourage money from the pockets of the spectators into the carnival coffers, and from there to support the clubs and local charities. At the largest of these carnivals, the reality is that on average, each spectator will contribute about 15p. This has to be the most disheartening aspect of carnival and spectators are encouraged to contribute at least £1 each.

In recent years, grand stand seating has been introduced and herein lies a more effective means of raising funds. Perhaps this is the way forward. Perhaps in forty or fifty years we will see all-seater procession routes, along the lines of the Jersey Battle of Flowers.

Perhaps in forty or fifty years, we will see generators which are so small, that the last 25% of a float's overall length won't be taken up by a large decorated box. Perhaps we will see the overall length of floats increase through the introduction of smaller units which can seamlessly join together, without the need for tow bars, in the procession. It is difficult to imagine what the future may bring. If we look back just one hundred years, we can see how carnival has changed beyond recognition. As the years pass the pace of change increases. I look forward to the future with excitement and enthusiasm.

PART 10
Bibliography and Acknowledgements

The author wishes to acknowledge the following for their invaluable help.

Malcolm (Dinger) Bell, Don Clifford, Kelly Coe, Stuart Davis, Nancy Dodds, Ena Hawins, David Kirk, Jnr., Anne Middleton, Keith 'Mini' Sheppard, Dave Squires, Rod Stoodley, Brian Seal, Phil Sealey, Pat Thick, Dee Thompson, John Thompson, Rai Turk and especially Brendon Hill (carnival historian) who provided such a useful wealth of archive material.

Bibliography
Hill, Brendon, *Everyone's a Winner*, (1996), Bridgwater, Brendon Hill.
Evans, Roger, *Bridgwater with and without the 'e'*, (1995), Bridgwater, Roger Evans.
Fraser, Antonio, *Faith and Treason – The Story of the Gunpowder Plot*, (1996), New York, Doubleday.

Photographic acknowledgements
All photos are the work of Peter J. Nicholls with the following exceptions:
Courtesy www.bridgwater-photos.co.uk: Page 86 (bottom)
From the collection of Mrs Ena Hawkins: Pages 12 (bottom), 48, 58, 64 and 93.
From the collection or originals of Roger Evans: Pages 9-10, 12 (top), 13-32, 34, 36, 41, 51-52, 56-57, 60, 66, 82 (bottom), 88, 96, 108-109 (top), 119, 127 and 154 (top).